HEARTS OF GOLD

Reflections of

COMMUNITY

Gold Award Girl Scouts

Sheryl M Robinson

Copyright Page

© 2026 Sheryl M Robinson
All rights reserved.

This book contains stories based on interviews with Gold Award Girl Scouts. "Girl Scout," "Girl Scouts," and "Gold Award" are registered trademarks of Girl Scouts of the USA, used in alignment with trademark guidelines for describing Girl Scouts.

Published by Grow and Share Network, LLC
First Edition, 2026

ISBN: 978-1-972135-06-8

Printed in the United States of America

Books in the Hearts of Gold Series

- *Earth Guardian*
- *STEM*
- *Creative Voice*
- *Health*
- *Inclusion*
- *Advocacy*
- *Community Connector*

Table of Contents

Chapter 1
What Community Is
From Observation to Action

Community connection often begins in the quietest moments of observation, when a young person notices a gap between how their town is and how it should be. One narrative in this book follows the theme of guarding memories, inspired by a girl who realized the local veterans she visited were waiting for a connection, not just the cookies she delivered. She stepped inside their homes and discovered a living archive of dusty scrapbooks and faded clippings, realizing that this history was not written in any textbook. The challenge was that these precious memories were fragile threads about to be lost forever because almost no one had ever asked these heroes about their service. To bridge the gap between generations, she decided to map the memories by creating an 84-page physical book and a digital archive of audio recordings. By turning tapes into truth, she ensured that the distinguished stories of the past were not silenced by the passage of time. Her growth was evident in her transition from a quiet fiction writer to a confident public speaker who could address town boards with grace, proving that the greatest way to honor the past is to listen to the present.

This pattern of moving from a witness to a leader is a common thread among the stories you will encounter. Another theme involves protecting the vulnerable, where a girl watched a stray cat seek sanctuary in her family's kayaks to give birth to her kittens. She realized there was a gap in advocacy for these community cats and initially faced rejection and redirection when a committee turned down her first, overly ambitious project ideas. She learned to pivot her frustration into a cause aligned with her true passions, discovering that rejection can be a form of redirection. Her action involved engineering high-quality, waterproof homes to protect these cats from the intense heat and rain of the Florida summer. Her impact was felt across a university campus, where she educated her peers on how to care for their neighbors and support stressed students' mental health. Her growth came from realizing that being alone is not what humanity is meant for, leading her to become a mentor to younger girls and a leader in her university community. These stories show that whether it is preserving history or protecting silent creatures, the impact begins when a girl decides her voice has the power to change the social fabric of her world.

Pulse of Modern Progress

In a rapidly changing world, building a community means ensuring that no one is left behind in a civic drought. One story explores the realization that even the best intentions can go astray when volunteers feel disconnected from their mission. One leader noticed peers hiding in the shadows of a food bank to avoid work, realizing they viewed service as a boring chore rather than an opportunity. Her action was to build a bridge to belonging by creating virtual volunteer fairs that matched students with organizations based on their specific career interests, such as engineering or marketing. This innovation transformed teens hiding behind crates into future leaders invested in their community's pulse. Despite facing a mountain of self-doubt and a cloud of procrastination, she learned that a leader is someone who listens to those who encourage them, eventually creating a permanent digital resource for youth development.

Similarly, a food pantry story highlights how engineering can be a tool for community inclusion and safety. This narrative follows a girl with a deep family history of service at a local food pantry who noticed that the pantry's heart was strong, but its tools were showing their age. The challenge was that the elderly volunteers were performing physically taxing work, often bending low to interact with heavy bags of food on a conveyor belt. Her action was to orchestrate a blueprint for better by designing and constructing a custom-engineered stand to raise the conveyor belt to an ergonomic height. She also launched the pantry's first digital presence, using a virtual handshake on social media to ensure the organization would no longer be a hidden gem. Her growth was found in her transition from a child carrying cans to a recognized community organizer who proved that persistence is the most valuable tool a leader can have. Through these innovations, these advocates show that a girl with a plan can turn a civic desert into a thriving garden of opportunity.

Constructing Digital Bridges

Connection often requires us to fine-tune our signal amidst the digital fog of modern life. You will meet a podcaster who navigated a long walk to leadership after moving through five or six different troops as her peers lost interest. Realizing that high school life can feel like an inner bubble of isolation, she decided to mic-check her own fears to create a podcast titled Thoughts for Your Thoughts. Her action involved becoming a digital architect, building a platform from the ground up to bridge the gap between global news and teenage mental health. She had to master the audio and overcome a cloud of procrastination, learning that it is okay to step back for a minute to assess the situation. Her impact was measured by hundreds of feedback cards from peers who felt high school was less scary because of her voice. She proved that leadership is about fine-tuning your signal until you break through the static of doubt, transforming a bridge of sound into a future career in political journalism.

In a world where media moves faster than the instructions for using it, we learn how a stamp can make an impact. This story begins in the silence of a pandemic, where a girl notices the heavy weight of isolation and a habit of doomscrolling. Realizing she had never written a letter in her life, she decided to prepare for her future military career by teaching others how to build real, lasting friendships without Wi-Fi. Her action was to act as a social architect, matching 180 girls across the country—and even a girl on a Navy base in Japan—based on their shared hobbies and personalities. She spent hours drawing personalized animals on postcards, proving that a piece of paper and a stamp could be more powerful than a text message. Her growth was found in the discipline of the letters across the ocean that sustained her through the silence of army boot camp. These digital architects show that, whether through an audio file or an envelope, a girl can build a bridge of communication that spans the digital frontier.

Finding a Verse of Belonging

True community is found when we create a sanctuary within the storm for those going through unimaginable hardships. We follow a girl who learned that childhood trauma can deeply impact a child's ability to learn and feel safe. Her action was to build a sanctuary of stories at a local shelter for families escaping domestic violence, creating a book nook where children could temporarily leave their troubles behind. Despite the challenges of a pandemic that left school hallways empty, she mobilized a book brigade, partnering with the National Honor Society to collect over 400 books. She persevered through the quiet climb of reports and unanswered emails, proving that true strength is about the willingness to finish what you start. Her impact was a permanent window of hope for children who needed to feel like heroes instead of victims.

Other narratives in this book explore how the spoken word and rhythm can create a verse of belonging. You will read about the Poet Laureate who noticed that, while her own voice was celebrated, many of her peers felt they lacked a platform to share their verses. Her action was to build a space for the silenced, leading workshops where girls could explore their identities through poetry without fear of judgment. She managed the professional publishing of a collective book, proving that if a girl can master a metaphor, she can master the confidence to speak up in a boardroom. Alongside her, a musician encountered a startling silence at her trade school, which lacked an arts budget. Her action was to orchestrate the logistics of a cross-district partnership, busing students between towns to create a unified symphony. She learned that leadership is a harmony of persistence through discordant notes, ensuring no future student had to choose between a trade and their love for music. These stories prove that when we open our hearts, we can turn a single stanza into a symphony of hope.

Designing for Inclusion

Finally, a strong community is one where every mind has a seat at the table and every neighbor is seen and fed. We learn empathy from a girl whose life is shaped by observing her brother's journey with autism. She noticed a troubling gap in her community where neurodiverse students were often pushed aside in social settings due to a minefield of anxiety and misunderstanding. Her action was to create Abilities with Possibilities, a specialized craft group at her local library that brought together neurotypical and neurodiverse worlds. She acted as an architect of empathy, designing a predictable routine that reduced anxiety and allowed participants to communicate through the shared language of art. Her growth was found in her transition from a sister to a community organizer and future legal advocate, proving that a leader is someone who makes others try.

This foundation is completed by a girl who began volunteering at a homeless shelter at just six years old. She noticed the mystery of peanut butter and pasta—the confusion on the faces of families who received random pantry items they didn't know how to cook. Her action was to test 60 flavors, researching and writing a professional cookbook focused on pantry staples. She overcame a lack of communication from organizations and pivoted her recipes to meet strict nutrition guidelines. Her impact created a global ripple effect, transforming her local project into a nonprofit called Young Chefs STL with chapters as far away as India and Canada. Her growth was found in her resilience through four-month lulls and her transition into a future environmental policy maker. Together, these advocates prove that when you combine a girl's vision with the courage to lead, you can cook up a future where no one is left hungry, and every voice is heard. This book is your roadmap of how a single observation can grow into a sustainable movement, proving that your ideas are worth it.

Chapter 2
Frequency of Change

Lindsey Pacela (Ep 25)

Long Walk to Leadership

Lindsey Pacela's story did not start with a microphone or a professional editing suite; it began in the simple, joyful world of a kindergarten classroom where she first joined Girl Scouts. For Lindsey, being a girl in this community meant more than just meeting once a week; it was a thirteen-year journey that shaped her entire perspective on the world. In the early years, the experience centered on the simple things, like eating cookies after school and singing songs while holding hands with friends. It was a time of pure fun and community service, but as the years went by, the world around her began to change. As Lindsey moved through elementary and middle school, she noticed that many of her peers were losing interest. People grew up, their schedules filled with other activities, and they began to leave the troop because they no longer thought being a Girl Scout was cool.

Lindsey faced many crossroads during those years. She moved through five or six different troops as groups disbanded or drifted apart. At one point, she was even driving an hour to reach a meeting spot because there were no other girls in her immediate area who were still involved. She admitted that there were moments when she wanted to give up, too. She wondered why she was the only one still walking this path when everyone else had stopped. However, her mother encouraged her to keep going, reminding her that she truly enjoyed the work and the impact she was making. Lindsey decided to stay, and that decision led her to the best troop experience of her life during her high school years.

One of the most defining moments of this community bond occurred during an overnight camping trip at Long Beach. Lindsey and her troop were lucky enough to use a beach house for a weekend event that drew nearly two hundred girls together. It was a period of high stress for many of them, as they were in the middle of studying for their high school finals. Instead of letting the pressure crush them, they spent the night on the sand, sharing snacks and giggling until one in the morning. Lindsey realized that these "giggly moments" were the true heart of her community. Having those moments of connection helped her realize that she wanted to create a platform where others could find that same sense of understanding and support. This long walk through different troops and experiences gave Lindsey the resilience she needed to launch a mission that would eventually broadcast her voice to the world.

Mic Check

As Lindsey entered her senior year of high school, she knew she wanted her project to reflect her deepest passions: journalism and politics. She had spent three years working on her high school yearbook, learning the art of storytelling and the importance of documenting the world around her. She felt a strong pull toward creating something that would educate and inspire others, but she faced a personal challenge. While she was very comfortable interviewing others and capturing their stories, she found the idea of her own voice being broadcast a little strange and intimidating. She preferred audio over video because it felt less like being in the spotlight and more like having a conversation in a safe space.

This realization led to the birth of her project, a podcast titled "Thoughts for Your Thoughts". Lindsey envisioned a program that would bridge the gap between complex global issues and teenagers' everyday lives. She decided that her podcast would focus on four essential pillars: world news, politics, high school life, and mental health. She believed that by connecting these topics, she could help her peers look outside their "inner bubble" and understand how they fit into the larger global community. It wasn't just about giving her own opinions; it was about providing audio education that would help listeners grow and think creatively.

Building the foundation for the podcast required a strong team, and Lindsey knew she couldn't do it alone. She recruited three others to join her mission, including a co-host who went by Alex on the program. Alex became a vital partner, helping Lindsey look for reputable sources and providing much-needed moral support during the more difficult parts of the journey. They also brought on an audio editor and another teammate who focused on building their presence on social media platforms like Facebook and Twitter. Lindsey was the lead project manager, but she learned that a successful community project is like a radio broadcast—it requires many different frequencies working together to create a clear signal. Together, they began the intense process of researching and preparing for their first recordings, ensuring that facts and integrity would back every word they spoke.

Digital Architect

Executing a podcast was a masterclass in technical skill and professional development for Lindsey. She didn't just sit down and talk; she had to become a digital architect, building a platform from the ground up. She spent over eight hours in the initial research phase alone, learning about the microbiology of sound and the legal requirements for founding an online program. She discovered that being a leader meant being willing to learn complex new tools on the fly. She had to manage international-level logistics, balancing her schoolwork with the demands of producing a regular audio show.

The technical side of the project was a steep learning curve that required both patience and precision. To ensure her podcast reached its audience and maintained a professional standard, Lindsey focused on several key technical steps:

- **Mastering** the audio program Audacity to edit out the "ums," "buts," and "ors" that appear in everyday speech to create a polished final product.
- **Constructing** a professional website using the Squarespace platform required her to research and perform basic coding to make the site functional.
- **Utilizing** a social media strategy that created a "domino effect," starting with friends and family and growing to reach a wider audience online.
- **Coordinating** with teachers from her high school and former junior high to schedule times for her podcast to be played in classrooms.

The audio editing process was particularly difficult. Lindsey spent hours listening to every minute of her recordings, realizing for the first time how much people repeat themselves or use filler words. While the work was tedious, she found it one of the most rewarding parts of the project because it taught her to listen more deeply. She recognized that every small edit was a step toward a better version of her message.

As the podcast grew, Lindsey also had to manage the challenge of setting up her digital presence. The website took nearly a month to put together, as she struggled with the "ins and outs" of web design. She learned that if she wanted people to take her message seriously, her digital storefront had to look as professional as the audio sounded. By the time she was ready to distribute her work to the classrooms, she had transformed from a student with an idea into a media producer who understood the mechanics of the digital frontier. She had proven that with enough research and a dedicated team, a girl could build a bridge of communication that spanned across the internet and into the hearts of her peers.

Cloud of Procrastination

Even the most dedicated leaders face moments of doubt, and Lindsey was no exception. About a quarter of the way through her project, she hit a mental wall. The sheer number of hours required for the project began to feel like a cloud hanging over her head. She started to feel scared and unsure if she had picked the right path. She wondered if she was doing the right thing and whether she could reach the finish line. This internal struggle is something many girls experience, but Lindsey found the strength to push through it during one of her own podcast interviews.

She invited a guest, Vicki, onto the show to discuss the psychology of procrastination. During the interview, Vicki explained that people often procrastinate because they are afraid of the task ahead or because they aren't finding joy in the process. Vicki emphasized that everyone needs to take breaks and that it is okay to step back for a minute to assess the situation. Lindsey realized that Vicki's words were speaking directly to her own heart. She took that advice to heart and learned to breathe, looking back at how far she had already come rather than focusing only on how much work remained.

The challenges weren't just internal; there were external hurdles as well. As she neared the end of her project, she struggled with the timing of feedback from the schools. She had played her podcast in several classrooms and was waiting for the teachers to send her feedback so she could document her project's impact. Some of the letters didn't arrive until the very last minute, which added significant stress to her final report. She learned that being a leader means rolling with the punches and staying persistent even when others aren't moving as fast as you are.

Lindsey reflected on these struggles during her exit interview and realized that she wouldn't have changed a single thing. She understood that the hard work of editing and the moments of doubt were all essential parts of her growth as a person. She realized that the journey to the goal line was just as important as the award itself. By overcoming procrastination and the stress of deadlines, she became a stronger, more confident version of herself than the girl who had started the project. She was now a role model for other first-year students who might be struggling with their own "what-ifs" in high school.

Echoes of Understanding

A physical measure of Lindsey's success was the stack of feedback cards she received from students who listened to her podcast. After visiting numerous classrooms, she collected between 200 and 300 notes from her peers. One anonymous student wrote that the podcast helped them realize that high school "won't be so scary," which meant the world to Lindsey. Another student shared that the episode on world news and the Hong Kong protests inspired them to look beyond their own "inner bubble" and pay attention to what was happening in the rest of the world. Knowing that she had touched lives and helped people feel less alone was the ultimate reward for her 80 hours of work.

Lindsey's project didn't just end with a final report; it set the stage for her entire future. She was accepted to La Verne University, where she decided to double major in journalism and political science. Her experience with the podcast and her years in yearbook gave her the confidence to pursue a career as a political journalist or a writer. But her ambitions went even higher than that. Inspired by her work in her community, Lindsey decided that she wanted to run for her local school district board one day. She wanted to be the person making the positive changes and impacts in students' lives that her teachers and mentors had made for her.

Lindsey discovered that leadership is like the frequency of a radio wave: you keep fine-tuning your signal until you break through the static of doubt. Her project was more than just an audio file; it was a bridge of sound that allowed students to cross over their fears and into a world of greater understanding. Lindsey took the cold facts of world news and the hard realities of mental health and made them soft and accessible for everyone brave enough to listen. She is a reminder that the most powerful echoes in our community are those that start with a single girl willing to say, "I have something to share."

Chapter 3
Pantry's New Pulse

Celestina Pint (Ep 80)

Heart Of Knoxville

For Celestina Pint, the city of Knoxville was not just a collection of streets and buildings, but a network of people who looked out for one another. Her journey into the world of service began so early that she could not even pinpoint the exact day it started. She had been volunteering at the West Knox Fish Pantry for as long as she could remember. As a young girl, she watched her father serve as the board treasurer, which gave her a unique, behind-the-scenes look at how a community resource operates. This deep family connection rooted her in the belief that feeding the community was a vital mission. She spent years helping carry bags and sorting cans, but as she grew older, she began to see the pantry through a different lens.

She noticed that while the heart of the pantry was strong, some of its physical and digital tools were starting to show their age. The pantry was a bustling place where volunteers worked tirelessly to ensure no neighbor went hungry. However, Celestina saw how to make the environment much safer and more efficient for everyone involved. She realized that for the pantry to keep serving Knoxville for many more years, it needed a serious update. This personal motivation came from her respect for the older volunteers who had dedicated their lives to this work. She wanted to provide them with a space that respected their effort and protected their health.

Celestina decided that her Gold Award would focus on revamping the pantry from the inside out. She didn't just want to paint a wall; she wanted to create a sustainable system that would help new volunteers find their way. Her project was born out of a desire to connect the generations of Knoxville through the shared language of kindness. She felt a profound responsibility to use her voice and her energy to strengthen the foundation of a place that had helped shape her own character. With a clear vision and a heart full of history, she prepared to lead a team through a transformation that would pulse through the entire community. She understood that a girl with a plan could be the bridge that ensures a local resource thrives for future generations.

Blueprint For Better

Once Celestina had identified the West Knox Fish Pantry's needs, she began the daunting task of planning the physical renovations. She knew that a deep cleaning was the first essential step to making the space feel refreshed and welcoming. She gathered a team of volunteers from her church, friends, and family. Together, they stood at the starting line of a mission that would require many hours of sweat and dedication. Celestina had to act as the lead project manager, coordinating everyone's schedules and ensuring they had the right supplies. She spent time researching the best materials for the floor and walls to ensure durability.

The most impressive part of the physical plan involved a specific piece of machinery that the pantry relied on every day: the conveyor belt. The volunteers used this belt to move heavy bags of food along a line where they filled them with cans and supplies. Celestina noticed that the elderly volunteers often had to bend down very low to interact with the bags, which was physically taxing. She decided to design and build a brand-new stand for the conveyor belt that would raise it to a more ergonomic height. To ensure professional precision for the project, she followed a specific sequence:

- **Orchestrated** a massive deep-cleaning day where her team scrubbed and painted the pantry walls and floors from top to bottom.
- **Constructed** a custom-engineered stand for the conveyor belt to ensure elderly volunteers did not have to bend down to load food.
- **Installed** new light fixtures and replaced broken shelving units to increase the overall safety and functionality of the workspace.

The process of building the stand was a major learning experience for Celestina. She had to rely on the advice of current volunteers who knew the process of bagging food inside and out. She

learned that the timing of these renovations was
critical because the pantry had to remain
operational. She worked with the staff to plan the
work for a time when the pantry had the least food
inventory. This step prevented renovations from
disrupting the pantry's daily operations and
ensured the community's food supply was never at
risk. She was learning that leadership is about
more than just building things; it is about respecting
the rhythm of the community you are trying to help.

By the time the last coat of paint was dry, and the
new lights were flicked on, the pantry's interior was
unrecognizable. The space felt safer, brighter, and
much more functional. The elderly volunteers were
especially vocal in their gratitude, noting that the
new conveyor stand was a game-changer for their
backs. Celestina had successfully turned her
research into a physical reality that improved the
lives of her fellow volunteers. She had proven that
a girl could manage a complex construction project
and lead a diverse team toward a common goal.
The physical blueprint was complete, and now it
was time for her to build the digital bridge.

Virtual Handshake

With the physical space renovated, Celestina
turned her attention to the digital world. She
realized that for the West Knox Fish Pantry to
attract new volunteers and reach more people in

need, it needed a modern online presence. Before her project, the pantry had almost no digital footprint, making it difficult for younger generations to find information about it. Celestina decided to change that by launching the pantry's first official social media accounts. She created a Facebook page and an Instagram account, giving the community a virtual window into the pantry's work. The organization's social media presence made it more visible and accessible than ever before.

She committed to updating these accounts at least once a month with pictures from the pantry and seasonal messages. She wanted the community to see the faces of the people they were helping and the dedicated volunteers who made it possible. Beyond social media, Celestina took on the major challenge of designing a custom website for the pantry. She filled the site with information about the organization's history, mission, and how it all started. The website became a permanent resource where people could learn how to donate or sign up to volunteer. She was using technology to build a bridge between the pantry and the wider Knoxville area.

To ensure the new digital presence was useful, Celestina also revamped the pantry's internal resources. She designed a comprehensive volunteer manual that streamlined the entire process of bagging and delivering food. This manual made it much easier for recruits to know exactly what to do from their very first day. She also developed nutritional recommendations and a poster guide for food bagging to ensure that every family received a balanced, well-organized supply bag. Her goal was to help the pantry stay organized and connected for years to come.

Celestina's work had immediate results. The pantry saw increased visibility, and the streamlined manual helped volunteers move through the process more quickly. Celestina was acting as an enabler of change, showing the pantry how to leverage technology to expand its reach. She had to learn how to explain her ideas to the board and get their approval for her social media posts. This process taught her about the importance of professional communication and collaboration. She realized that a girl's voice could help an older organization adapt to a new era. Through her digital work, she ensured that the West Knox Fish Pantry would never be a hidden gem again.

Navigating The Obstacle Course

Even with her deep history at the pantry, the road to completing her project was not without its detours and obstacles. One of Celestina's biggest initial fears was that she would not be able to find enough people to help her with the renovations. She knew that painting a floor and building a machine stand were too much for one girl to do alone. She reached out to her church and shared her mission, hoping that people would be willing to give up their free time. To her surprise, the church posted the sign-up information on their Facebook page, and the response was overwhelming. She ended up with more than enough volunteers, proving that when a girl asks for help for a good cause, the community will show up.

Another major challenge Celestina faced was the organization's timeline. The group of volunteers who managed the pantry only met quarterly, so she often had to wait months before the group would make major decisions. There were moments when she felt slowed down by this schedule, as she was eager to keep the momentum going. However, she learned to adapt her own schedule to theirs, realizing that leadership requires patience and the ability to work within existing structures. She used these waiting periods to refine her manual and her nutritional posters, ensuring that every detail was perfect before the next meeting.

The physical work of the renovations also tested her endurance. Scrubbing and painting the pantry was tiring work that took many long hours. Celestina admitted that it was one of the most difficult parts of the journey, but she found joy in doing it alongside her team. She learned that being a leader meant being the one to pick up the paintbrush first and stay until the last volunteer went home. She turned her challenges into

opportunities for growth, realizing that every
obstacle was just a step toward her final
destination. She had to keep her ducks in a row
and stay organized despite the slow quarterly
meetings.

Reflecting on these challenges, Celestina realized
that she had gained a new level of self-confidence.
She had managed a diverse team, navigated local
government-style board meetings, and completed a
major construction and digital overhaul. She
understood that she could do amazing things when
she remained dedicated to her why. Her journey
through the project's obstacle course had
transformed her from a quiet volunteer into a
recognized community organizer. She proved that
persistence is the most valuable tool a leader can
have.

Legacy Of A Leader

The impact of Celestina's project was both visible
and measurable, as evidenced by volunteers'
smiles and the pantry's efficiency. She had
implemented modernization and safety, a move
that resonated throughout West Knoxville. The
pantry was now safer, more visible, and better
equipped to handle new volunteers. For Celestina,
finishing the project felt like the completion of a
major chapter in her life, taking her from a five-
year-old child carrying cans to a young woman who

had engineered a community solution. Her project had reached hundreds of people, ensuring that the legacy of kindness she had grown up with would continue to flourish.

Her leadership growth during the project set the stage for a future dedicated to science and discovery. She realized, after 80-plus hours of work, that she enjoyed the process of problem-solving and research. The project led her to set a goal of majoring in biomedical engineering in college, where she hopes to conduct research that will help people worldwide. She also remains a girl at heart, continuing to enjoy her favorite outdoor activities, such as backpacking and wilderness camping. Her project taught her to balance a busy school schedule with meaningful service, a skill she will use throughout her life.

Celestina's advice to other girls considering their own project is to put a lot of effort into the paperwork. She believes that if you write a meaningful proposal and final report, the interviews and the execution will be much easier. She encourages girls to choose a topic they believe in, as she did with the pantry, so that the work never feels like a chore. She has transformed from a shy student into a vocal advocate. Celestina Pint is a reminder that when we decide to connect our community, we don't just fix a building; we strengthen the heart of our town.

Celestina discovered that leadership is like renovating a tired space: it requires a vision of what could be, the strength to scrub away the old, and the heart to paint a brighter future. Her project was more than just a conveyor stand or a website; it was a warm flame that helped melt the barriers of inefficiency and silence in her community.

Celestina took the heat of her challenges and used them to fuse a solid legacy of service. She is a reminder that the most durable things we build are the connections we make when we decide to stand up and say that every neighbor deserves to be seen and fed.

Chapter 4
Open Your Heart

Savannah Garrett (Ep 92)

Sanctuary Of Stories

Savannah Garrett began her life of service at only five years old, entering a world of sisterhood that would define the next 14 years of her life. She grew up with the same troop leader, Miss Phelps, and a small group of friends who became as close as family. They shared countless nights at camp, staying awake until 3:00 a.m., giggling in their tents while the adults told them to be quiet. Through these years, Savannah learned a vital lesson: community isn't just about where you live; it's about how you support those around you. As she entered high school, she began to look at the world with a more critical eye, searching for a way to use her voice to help those overlooked.

A late-blooming love for reading fueled her journey toward her project. While she admits that she often felt forced to read as a young child, as she grew older, she discovered that books were more than just school assignments. She realized that for children going through unimaginable hardships, a book could be a life-saving escape. Through her research, Savannah learned that childhood trauma can deeply impact a child's ability to learn, making them more easily distracted and less likely to grasp new information in class. She felt a deep, personal motivation to create a space where these children could feel safe and understood.

Savannah decided to focus her efforts on the intake center of a local shelter for women and children escaping domestic violence, an organization called Aid to Victims of Domestic Violence (AVDA). She knew that when a family arrives at a shelter, the mothers are often overwhelmed with paperwork and difficult conversations. During those heavy moments, the children need to wait, feeling the weight of the stress around them. Savannah envisioned a book nook as a sanctuary within the storm. In this place, a child could "snuggle up with a bean bag, a book, and a blanket" and temporarily leave their troubles behind to explore a far-away land through the eyes of a character.

Blueprint Of Belief

Starting a project of this magnitude was an exercise in focus and determination. Savannah quickly realized that having total creative freedom was a blessing and a curse. While she could address any issue she felt passionate about, narrowing down her big ideas into a single, workable plan was a major challenge. She spent weeks brainstorming, worrying whether her ideas were big enough or would truly make a difference. However, the encouragement of Miss Phelps and her mother kept her moving forward. They reminded her that every huge achievement begins with a single, small decision to try.

To turn her vision into a reality, Savannah had to step into the role of a professional researcher and community liaison. She didn't just want to drop off a few boxes of books; she wanted to build something that would last. She reached out to AVDA and connected with Ginger Pool, who became her primary resource at the shelter. Together, they identified the perfect spot in the intake center for the book nook. Savannah understood that the stakes were high; research showed that children from single-parent homes or traumatic backgrounds were more likely to drop out of school early. By fostering a love of reading in the shelter, she wasn't just providing entertainment; she was building a foundation for their future education.

Savannah's planning process was meticulous. She knew she needed at least 80 hours of dedicated work to see the project through to its official completion. She had to coordinate between the shelter, her school, and her team of volunteers. This stage of the journey taught her that leadership isn't just about giving orders; it's about building a bridge between people who want to help and those who need it most. She began to view her project to connect her own stable community with a community in crisis, ensuring that the children at AVDA knew the world did not forget them outside the shelter walls.

Mobilizing The Book Brigade

The project required Savannah to transform from a student into a logistics manager and a builder. Because her project took place in 2021, she had to navigate the strange reality of a world still recovering from a pandemic. Many students weren't physically in school, which made her plan to collect books even more difficult. However, she refused to let the empty hallways stop her. She partnered with her high school's National Honor Society, setting up a collection point where students could drive by and drop off their donations.

Savannah was stunned by the overwhelming response from her peers. Despite the challenges of the time, the community showed up with open hearts. To ensure the mission was a success, she and her team followed a very specific set of implementation steps:

- They **partnered** with the National Honor Society to collect over 400 books, blankets, and stuffed animals from students who drove to the school specifically to donate to the cause.
- They **constructed** and hand-painted a large, sturdy bookcase, adding a bright rainbow on the side to brighten the intake center's atmosphere.

- They **curated** each donation to ensure every book and toy was in good condition, so the children receiving them felt respected and cared for.
- They **launched** a dedicated website that provided book recommendations and allowed users to suggest new titles to add to the Nook in the future.

The physical work was exhausting but deeply rewarding. Savannah's boyfriend, Ethan, helped her sort through the mountain of books, while her friend, Maddie, helped her paint the rainbow on the bookcase. Even her mother joined in, helping her shove a big bookcase into the back of their car so they could drive it to the shelter. Seeing the bookcase fill up with colorful stories was the visible proof of what a group of dedicated people could achieve. Savannah had successfully connected her high school community with the families at AVDA, proving that books are a powerful currency of care.

Quiet Climb

Even with a garage full of books and a beautiful bookcase, Savannah faced a difficult internal battle: the challenge of perseverance. As a girl who liked to see results immediately, the slow pace of a long-term project was a test of her spirit. "I'm the kind of person who once I get really excited about something, I just want it to get done right at that second," she explained. But her project wasn't something that could be finished in a weekend. It required months of steady effort, constant communication, and patience as official approvals and paperwork were processed.

The quiet moments of the project—the times spent writing reports, sending emails that went unanswered for days, and managing the 80-hour timeline—were the hardest parts of the climb. There were days when she felt discouraged, wondering if the impact would be as large as she hoped. However, Savannah learned to stay encouraged by remembering the children who would eventually use the nook. She realized that her willingness to persist through the boring or difficult parts was what would ultimately make the project successful. She had to learn to stay passionate even when the initial excitement had worn off.

This period of growth changed Savannah's perspective on leadership. She realized that true strength isn't just about making a big splash at the beginning; it's about the willingness to persevere until the very end. She leaned on the own it philosophy she had heard from an older girl years before—the idea that you should be proud to be a Girl Scout, no matter what others might say. By the time the book nook was installed at the AVDA intake center, Savannah had reached her goal. She had proven to herself that she could finish a massive project, even when the path got rocky or the destination seemed far away.

Beyond The Last Page

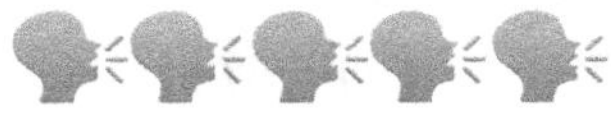

The impact of "Open Your Heart, Open a Book" rippled through the community in ways Savannah never expected. After finishing the project, she received a wave of recognition that she described as shocking. Her local newspaper wrote an article about her work and featured it on social media pages. While she was grateful for the praise, the most meaningful feedback came from the shelter itself, where the children were finally using the sanctuary she had built. Savannah had given them a permanent resource—a bridge to a world where they could feel like heroes instead of victims.

Savannah attends the University of Central Florida, studying political science with a focus on national intelligence and security. She plans to take the lessons of her project with her to Washington, D.C., where she hopes to work with the government to continue making the world a better place. Her advice to other girls is simple: "Be yourself... know that your voice matters". She encourages everyone to never give up on their dreams, because they are absolutely achievable if you are willing to put in the work.

Savannah's journey is a reminder that a community is like a well-loved book: there are many different stories, and some are harder to read than others. When we find a chapter of our community that is struggling or in pain, we have the power to be the authors of a better ending. Savannah didn't just build a bookcase; she built a window of hope, proving that when one girl decides to open her heart, she can help an entire community find the strength to turn the page and start a brand-new story.

Chapter 5
Bridges of Ink and Paper

Hannah Crawley (Ep 155)

Screen and the Silence

In the quiet suburbs of South Texas, Hannah Crawley sat in her room, staring at the blue light of her phone. Outside, the world had slowed to a crawl. It was the height of the pandemic, and like millions of other teenagers, Hannah felt the heavy weight of isolation. A digital fog had replaced the usual buzz of school hallways and troop meetings. She found herself caught in the cycle of doom scrolling, a habit of just keeping her thumb sliding across the screen, looking at news and posts until her eyes got tired and her mind felt empty. She knew that while her phone kept her connected to the internet, it wasn't really keeping her connected to people.

Hannah started thinking about her future. She had always planned to follow in her father's and grandfather's footsteps by joining the military. But there was a problem. In the army, especially during basic training, you don't get to keep your cell phone. Communication happens the old-fashioned way: through letters. Hannah realized with a start that she had never written a letter in her life. She didn't know how the postal system worked, how to address an envelope, or how to say everything she wanted to say without an instant message or an emoji. It was a realization that sparked a huge idea.

If she was feeling lonely and disconnected, surely other girls were, too. She wanted to create a way for people to build real, lasting friendships that didn't rely on Wi-Fi. She imagined a project that would act as a bridge, connecting communities across the country through the simple act of writing. By teaching others how to send mail, she would be preparing herself for her military journey while helping hundreds of other girls find a friend in a time of darkness. She wanted to prove that a piece of paper and a stamp could be more powerful than a text message, because a letter is something you can hold in your hand and keep in a drawer forever.

Logic of the Stamp

Turning a big dream into a working project required more than just a pen; it required a serious team and a lot of organization. Hannah knew she couldn't do this alone. She recruited her mother and her friend's mother to help manage the complicated logistics of finding people. They used social media to create a group where parents could sign up their daughters. To her surprise, the message traveled fast. Soon, they had 180 girls signed up from all over the United States, and even one girl living all the way in Japan. Not just a local club anymore; the group was a nationwide network.

Hannah didn't want to just pair people up at random. She knew that if the friendships were going to last, the girls needed to have things in common. She spent hours reviewing the applications, reading about each girl's likes and hobbies. She acted like a social architect, carefully matching people based on their personalities. She also wanted to make sure the project felt like a community, so she organized monthly Zoom meetings. During these calls, the girls would work on patch programs together, keeping everyone engaged and excited about the next letter arriving in their mailbox.

To make sure every part of the program was successful, Hannah followed a very specific plan:

- **Identified** participants through a dedicated social media group to reach families across different states.
- **Coordinated** a matchmaking system that pairs girls based on shared hobbies and age.
- **Facilitated** monthly digital workshops to teach the history of the postal service and help girls earn creative patches.
- **Monitored** ongoing correspondence to ensure everyone is receiving responses and feels included.

By creating this structure, Hannah was able to manage the chaos. Her friends Celeste, Mercedes, and Adriana stepped up to help write letters when the workload became too much for one person to handle. They became a small factory of kindness, ensuring that every girl who sent a letter received a thoughtful response. Hannah learned that being a leader meant knowing when to ask for help and how to leverage your friends' strengths to reach a common goal. She was no longer just a student; she was the director of a pen pal empire that was bringing smiles to mailboxes from Texas to Minnesota.

The Puzzle of Personalization

Even with a great team, the project brought challenges that tested Hannah's patience. The biggest headache was the matchmaking process itself. As girls signed up, they had different requests. Some wanted a pen pal from their own state, while others wanted to talk to someone on the other side of the country. Every time a new person joined, or someone needed a new match, it was like a giant puzzle where moving one piece affected all the others. Hannah described it as having many moving parts that had to stay perfectly aligned. If she had just picked names out of a hat, it would have been easier, but she knew the heart of the project depended on those personal connections.

Another challenge was the physical work required to make the letters special. Hannah wanted the very first postcards to be more than just a hello. She decided to draw a personalized animal on every single card, based on what each girl liked. If a girl loved cats, Hannah drew a cat. If she loved dolphins, she drew a dolphin. She spent five straight hours sitting at her desk, drawing and coloring until her hand ached. It was a marathon of creativity that left her exhausted, but she kept going because she knew how much it would mean to the girls. She imagined them opening their mail and seeing a hand-drawn picture of their favorite animal, knowing that someone they had never met had taken the time to create it just for them.

Hannah also had to fight a personal battle against procrastination. Like many middle and high school students, she found it easy to put things off until the last minute. But with 180 people waiting for mail, she couldn't afford to be lazy. She watched as some of her friends in other troops struggled to finish their projects because they started too late and missed the deadline. Because Hannah and her mother had started planning back in eighth grade and launched it in ninth grade, she was able to finish her work without the stress of a ticking clock. This decision taught her the value of getting a head start, a lesson that helped her relax and support her friends with their own projects when they got overwhelmed.

Letters Across the Ocean

The most exciting part of the project was seeing how far the letters could travel. One of the most unique connections was with a girl named Reagan, who lived on a Navy base in Japan. Because Reagan was part of a military family, her mail could be sent through the military postal system, allowing her to participate in Hannah's program. The two girls became fast friends through their envelopes. They didn't just share stories; they shared a bit of their cultures. Reagan would send Hannah colorful Japanese candies that you couldn't find in Texas, and Hannah would send back spicy Mexican candies popular in her hometown.

This international friendship became a lifeline for both. Even when Hannah finally reached her goal and headed off to boot camp, the letters didn't stop. In the military, where you are often tired and far from home, mail call is the highlight of the day. Receiving a letter from Reagan or another pen pal reminded Hannah that there were people who cared about her and her journey. "It was nice to know that even when I was there, they still cared," she remembered. Those letters were a constant reminder of the community she had built, and they gave her the strength to push through the difficult training.

The project's measurable impact was clear: 180 girls had learned a new way to communicate. Even today, long after the official project ended, Hannah keeps up with twenty-two pen pals. She has a drawer full of letters from girls like Sophia and

Emma, keeping their stories tucked away like treasures. These weren't just temporary pandemic distractions; they were real connections that had survived the return to normal life. Hannah had successfully bridged the gap between different worlds, showing that whether you are in a small town in Texas or a Navy base in Japan, the human need for friendship and a kind word is the same.

Beyond the Envelopes

Today, Hannah is a long way from her South Texas bedroom. She is currently in the middle of her Advanced Individual Training (AIT) for the army, which she describes as the college portion of her military education. Her days are intensely structured, starting with physical training at four o'clock in the morning. She balances schoolwork, homework, and military drills, yet she still makes time to write letters. The project she started in high school prepared her perfectly for this life. She is now following in the footsteps of her father and grandfather, making her family proud as a strong, capable soldier.

Her leadership growth is also evident in how she talks about her time as a camp counselor. Using the camp name "Spooky" because of her love for Halloween, she mentored a group of younger girls, sharing stories about high school and encouraging them to find their own confidence. Even a scary midnight encounter with a porcupine during a trip to the nurse's office became a story of resilience. Hannah learned that being a leader is about taking that first step, even when you are nervous. "If you don't make the first step, then you're never going to get anywhere," she advised. She has learned to shoot her shot without second-guessing herself, a trait that has served her well in the army.

Looking toward the future, Hannah hopes for a long career in the military. But if she ever leaves the service, she wants to follow her mother's example of helping military families. She has seen how much her mother does to support others, and she wants to continue that legacy of service. Whether she is in uniform or in civilian clothes, Hannah knows she will always be a builder of communities. She has gone from a girl who didn't know how to address an envelope to a woman who leads with confidence and heart.

Hannah has allowed the challenges of her project and the discipline of the military to shape her into a leader who is both strong and compassionate. Her project was the first draft of a life dedicated to connecting people, and now, with every letter she writes and every drill she completes, she is finishing the story. She remains a reminder that when you put down the phone and pick up a pen, you can change the world one envelope at a time.

Chapter 6
Abilities with Possibilities

Maya Welber (Ep 19)

Quiet Power Of Connection

For Maya Welber, the world of special needs was never a foreign concept; it was the world she lived in every single day. Her journey toward leadership and community connection began right in her own living room, shaped by the life of her younger brother. He was diagnosed with autism when he was just three years old, a moment that changed the trajectory of Maya's childhood. While other children were busy with sports or playdates, Maya often sat in on her brother's therapy sessions. She wasn't just a bystander; she was a keen observer, watching and learning from speech therapists, occupational therapists, and specialists in applied behavior analysis. Through these experiences, Maya gained a unique perspective on the world. She saw firsthand that, while her brother viewed life through a different lens, his potential was limitless if given the right environment to bloom.

As Maya grew older, she noticed a troubling gap in her community of Newtown, Connecticut. She saw that as children move from elementary school into the high-stakes world of high school, the social landscape becomes much more difficult to navigate. For a neurotypical student, making friends and joining clubs is a standard part of the teenage experience. Still, for someone on the spectrum, those same situations can feel like a minefield of anxiety and misunderstanding. Maya watched her brother enter high school and realized how isolating it could be when you have difficulty being social. She began to worry about the bubble that often forms around children with special needs. They were frequently pushed aside in social settings, not because people were intentionally mean, but because their peers simply didn't know how to approach them.

This realization settled in her heart, sparking a personal motivation to act. She didn't want just to help her brother; she wanted to change the culture of her entire town. She believed that the root cause of the isolation was a lack of substantial resources available to those who were not on the spectrum. If she could find a way to bring these two worlds together—the neurotypical and the neurodiverse— she could foster a sense of acceptance that didn't yet exist. Maya realized she had a passion for helping people and a deep love for the arts, and she decided to combine these two forces into a mission to bridge the gap between different types of minds. She was ready to take the techniques she had learned in therapy rooms and bring them out into the public eye, proving that every child has possibilities worth exploring.

Blueprint For Inclusion

Designing a program that effectively integrates children of all abilities requires more than just a good heart; it requires a structured plan and a professional partnership. Maya knew that if her project was going to succeed, it needed a home that was welcoming to everyone. She turned to the C.H. Booth Library in Newtown, a place she already knew well because she worked there herself. She approached the library staff with her vision for a specialized craft group, and they were immediately supportive. They recognized that while the library had many programs, there was nothing specifically designed to create an integrated environment for neurotypical children and those on the spectrum. The library graciously agreed to fund the project, providing Maya with the foundation she needed to start building her blueprint.

Maya decided to name her initiative Abilities with Possibilities. The name itself was a statement of her belief that a disability should never define a person's potential. She spent five months meticulously planning the schedule and the curriculum. She knew that consistency was vital, especially for children on the spectrum who often thrive when they have a clear plan and a predictable routine. After years of helping her brother, Maya understood that knowing what is happening next provides a sense of safety. Therefore, she decided the group would meet once a month, always for a couple of hours on a Saturday afternoon. This strict adherence to a schedule allowed the participants and their families to plan, reducing the anxiety that often comes with new social experiences.

However, Maya also wanted to ensure that the environment was flexible enough to encourage true creativity. She didn't want the group to feel like another clinical therapy session; she wanted it to feel like a community. She spent hours researching projects on Pinterest and other creative platforms, looking for crafts that focused on fine motor skills—the very skills that occupational therapy works to improve. She wanted to provide a safe space where a child could choose to paint a birdhouse or, if they felt inspired, paint a picture of their mother instead. This blend of structure and freedom became the core of her project's design. She was acting as an architect of empathy, creating a space where children could meet peers who were different from them and realize that, at the end of the day, they all shared a love for creating something beautiful.

Brushes, Bridges, and Possibilities

When the first Saturday finally arrived, Maya's vision moved from a blueprint into a living, breathing reality. The library craft room was transformed into a hub of activity, filled with paint, glitter, and the excited chatter of children. Maya stood at the center of it all, no longer just a student, but a project manager leading a team of volunteers. She had to manage the logistics of setting up stations, welcoming families, and ensuring that every child felt seen and understood. The sessions weren't just about the finished crafts; they were about the interactions that happened over the paintbrushes. Maya watched as neurotypical children sat alongside those on the spectrum, realizing that they could communicate through the shared language of art.

The project's implementation was a lesson in delegation and community outreach. Maya realized that to make the program sustainable, she had to build a network of support that extended beyond the library walls. To ensure execution with professional precision, she followed a clear set of actions:

- **Partnered** with the C.H. Booth Library to secure a permanent location and a consistent source of funding for all craft materials.
- **Recruited** a dedicated team of volunteers, including peers from her school and fellow library staff, to provide one-on-one assistance to children during the sessions.
- **Developed** an intensive promotional strategy, utilizing both physical posters in local schools and digital outreach on social media platforms.

The impact of these sessions was immediate. Parents would drop their children off, grateful for a two-hour window of respite—a precious commodity for families of children with special needs. They felt supported knowing their child was in a welcoming environment rather than merely tolerated. Maya's role as the leader meant she had to be constantly aware of her participants' needs. If a child felt overwhelmed by the noise, she was there to help them find a quieter corner. If another child struggled with a specific tool, she used her knowledge of motor skills to show them a new technique. She was proving that leadership is about making others try.

The success of the Abilities with Possibilities group showed Maya that she could manage a complex community initiative. She was no longer just a sister trying to help her brother; she was a community organizer who had successfully started the conversation about inclusion in her town. Every painting that went home on a Saturday afternoon was a reminder that when you provide the right tools, everyone can contribute to the neighborhood's beauty. Maya realized that the most important thing she was building wasn't a craft; it was a bridge of understanding that would remain long after the paint had dried.

Spreading The Word In A Small Town

Despite the success of the sessions, Maya faced a significant hurdle that many young leaders encounter: promotion. In a very small town like

Newtown, getting the word around can be surprisingly difficult. Maya found that promoting was her biggest takeaway because it required her to step far outside her comfort zone. She couldn't just rely on her friends to show up; she had to find ways to reach families who had never heard of her group, which required a level of communication and public speaking entirely new to her. She had to become an advocate for her own work, pitching the importance of her mission to school officials and local media.

She decided to take a multi-pronged approach to marketing. She created custom tote bags and cinch bags with the Abilities with Possibilities logo to hand out at every meeting, turning her participants into walking ambassadors for the program. She also reached out to the local news department in her town for an interview. Standing in front of a camera and explaining the why behind her project was a nerve-wracking experience, but she knew it was necessary to reach a wider audience. The interview was eventually released and posted at the library, giving the program a new level of professional credibility. She also worked closely with occupational therapists at Newtown High School, asking them to share her project with families who might benefit from the group.

The external challenges matched the internal growth Maya experienced during this phase. She learned that being a leader means being persistent. When she didn't hear back from a contact immediately, she didn't take it personally; she sent a follow-up. She used her Instagram page to post regular updates and photos of the crafts, creating a digital record of the program's journey. By the time the first few months had passed, the word-of-mouth success was building a domino effect of interest. Maya realized that special needs is a spectrum and that no two participants would react the same way, requiring her to be constantly flexible and ready to pivot her plans at a moment's notice.

Reflecting on these challenges, Maya realized that her project was teaching her as much as she was teaching the children. She was building interpersonal skills that she knew she would use for the rest of her life. She was learning how to manage a team, relate to professionals, and hold her ground when things got rocky. The struggle to promote the group had given her the confidence to realize that she had a voice that people wanted to hear. She was no longer afraid to put herself out there because she saw that the results—the children's smiles and the parents' gratitude—were worth every moment of social anxiety. Maya had successfully broken through the small-town silence and made her mission a known entity in the community.

Future Built On Understanding

As Maya concluded her formal project report, the impact of her work was visible in the thriving community she had built. She had successfully integrated groups of neurotypical and neurodiverse children, fostering friendships that likely never would have formed otherwise. One of her favorite memories occurred during a painting session when a new little girl walked into the library. The girl didn't want to paint the scheduled craft; instead, she asked if she could paint a portrait of Maya. Her mother took a photo of the two of them with the painting, and in that moment, Maya realized the magnitude of what she had accomplished. She was a role model for these children, someone they looked up to and wanted to connect with. Parents felt supported, and the children felt empowered.

The growth Maya experienced through her project has set the stage for a future dedicated to advocacy. She realized, after 80+ hours of work, that she wanted to pursue a career in special needs advocacy and law. She wants to continue doing work that helps people socialize and find their place in a world that often feels unwelcoming. Her time in Girl Scouts, moving from the Silver Award to the Gold Award, has given her the confidence and the organizational skills to tackle any future challenge. She encourages other girls to stay in Girl Scouts and follow their passions, telling them that the journey of self-discovery is the most valuable reward.

Maya's unique personality and her history with her community shine through. She looks at traditional situations and finds a way to add her own possibility to make the outcome even more amazing. Whether doing crafts or planning a legal career, Maya Welber moves forward with the quiet confidence of someone who knows how to connect a community.

Maya discovered that leadership is like creating a complex craft: it requires a steady hand, a lot of patience, and the willingness to get a little messy along the way. Her project was more than just a series of library workshops; it was a warm flame that helped melt the cold barriers between children of different abilities. Maya took the raw materials of her community and blended them to create a legacy of understanding. She is a reminder that the most durable things we build are the connections we make when we decide to open our arms and say that every mind is full of possibilities.

Chapter 7
Symphony of Unity

Kelsey Aggrey (Ep 24)

Silence of the Trades

♫ ♫ ♫ ♫ ♫

Kelsey Aggrey always knew that music was her second language. Since her days in elementary school, she had found her voice through instruments and melody. For Kelsey, music wasn't just a hobby; it was a sanctuary that created lasting memories and brought a joy that words alone couldn't capture. As she grew older, she assumed that high school would be the place where her musical passion would reach its peak. However, when she enrolled as a senior at Monty Tech High School in Massachusetts, she encountered a startling silence.

Monty Tech was a trade school, a place where students were busy mastering plumbing, electrical work, cosmetology, and early childhood education. With a school budget heavily focused on providing the tools and technology needed for these specific trades, there simply wasn't room for a music program. There was no band, no choir, and no place for students to explore their artistic side through sound. Kelsey remembered feeling a profound sadness when she realized there was no musical background in her new environment at all. She didn't want any other student to feel that same void, and she believed that choosing a trade shouldn't mean giving up the love of music.

This personal realization became the driving force behind her Gold Award. She knew she wanted to include music in her project and that the community she wanted to impact was her own school. Her motivation was clear: she wanted to instill a love for music in a place where it had been forgotten. She believed that music was essential for everyone, regardless of their career path. Kelsey wasn't just looking for a way to play her own instrument; she was looking to connect with a community of silent musicians who were waiting for someone to start the rhythm. With a heart full of passion and a mind set on change, she prepared to pitch an idea that would bridge the gap between two different towns and two very different schools.

Building the Bridge of Sound

Turning the silence of a trade school into a symphony required Kelsey to look beyond her own hallways. She realized that if Monty Tech couldn't afford its own program, the answer might lie in a partnership. She decided to join forces with her principal to develop a realistic budget and a plan that would work. Together, they looked at Leominster High School, located just a few towns over. Leominster had an established band program, but it faced its own challenges. Their band wasn't as large as they'd hoped, and they were looking for a way to spark new interest among their own students.

Kelsey reached out to the band director at Leominster, Barry Hudson, and proposed a radical idea: combine the musical students from both schools into one unified ensemble. To her delight, Mr. Hudson was incredibly supportive. He saw it as a unity thing, a way for two communities to come together and become one. He opened his doors to the Monty Tech students, even offering to provide music and instruments for those who needed to borrow them. Kelsey was amazed at how quickly everything began to fall into place once she found a partner who shared her vision for music.

Before the rehearsals could begin, Kelsey had to ensure that the interest at Monty Tech was real. She organized a school-wide poll to ask her peers if they played instruments and if they would be interested in joining a combined band. To build excitement, she arranged for the Leominster High School band to visit Monty Tech and perform during the lunch periods. Seeing the band play in their own cafeteria allowed the trade students to see exactly what they could be a part of. The hallway conversations shifted from plumbing and engines to rhythm and scales. Kelsey was ready to move from planning to the complex task of orchestrating the logistics of a two-school operation.

Orchestrating the Logistics

Executing a project that involved transporting students between towns required Kelsey to become a master of professional communication and organization. She wasn't just a student musician anymore; she was a project manager overseeing a complex schedule that relied on buses, permission slips, and constant coordination between two administrations. She had to ensure that the Monty Tech students had a way to reach Leominster High School immediately after their school day ended and a way to get back home safely afterward. It was a massive undertaking that required her to be on top of her game every single day.

Kelsey's role as the leader made her the primary point of contact for everyone involved. She gave her phone number to dozens of people, and her phone was constantly buzzing with questions about upcoming events, instrument storage, and bus times. Her principal reminded her that she was responsible for guiding the guest students through the school, showing them where to go and even where the bathrooms were. She felt overwhelmed at times, but seeing herself in that leadership role was one of the most rewarding parts of the journey. She was learning that being a leader meant serving the group's needs.

To keep the mission running smoothly and ensure that both programs remained sustainable, Kelsey followed a very specific cycle of actions:

- **Organized** a recurring transportation system that used school buses to ferry musicians between Monty Tech and Leominster High School for weekly rehearsals.
- **Coordinated** with the Leominster band director to manage instrument loans and music distribution, ensuring no student was left out due to a lack of resources.
- **Promoted** the program through a series of grand opening-style lunch performances and informational polls to keep the student body engaged.
- **Managed** the communication between two separate school boards to secure the long-term permissions needed for a cross-district partnership.

The results of this hard work were visible in the creation of a unified concert band and a choir. They didn't just practice together; they performed together, holding winter and spring concerts at both schools. Instead of just one audience, the students now had two, doubling the impact of their music. Kelsey had transformed a trade school with no arts budget into a place where students could receive a hands-on trade education while also pursuing their love of music. By creating a system that didn't rely on a single school's massive budget, she proved that community connection is the most valuable resource of all.

Harmony of Persistence

Despite the beauty of the music, the project was not without its discordant notes. Kelsey's biggest challenge was maintaining the momentum and keeping the same group of people involved over the long term. While there was an initial wave of excitement, the reality of the logistics began to set in for some students. Some of her peers grew frustrated with the travel. They didn't want to be bused over to another school every day after a long day of trade classes; they wanted their own program right there at Monty Tech. Kelsey found it difficult to make everyone happy while working within the reality of the present moment.

She had to learn how to communicate the why behind the partnership. She explained to her upset peers that while the long-term goal might be a program at their own school, this partnership was the stage they were currently in. It was a lesson in managing expectations and staying patient when people were frustrated. Kelsey felt a personal weight because it was her project, and she felt responsible for the happiness of every participant. She had to roll with the punches and remain a steady voice of encouragement, even when she didn't have total control over the situation.

Through these trials, Kelsey discovered that leadership is often about persistence through the nos and the complaints. She stayed focused on her why—the freshman who would one day walk into Monty Tech and realize they didn't have to choose between a trade and a band. She used the skills she had gained to stay organized and dedicated. Whether it was dealing with the creepy but fun memories of visiting the Salem Witch Museum or the teamwork she learned while preparing dinner at camp, those experiences had built the grit she needed to see the music project through to its conclusion. Kelsey proved that a leader doesn't need to have all the answers; they just need the will to keep the music playing until the harmony returns.

Symphony That Never Ends

The impact of Kelsey's project was both immediate and long-lasting. By the time she graduated, the partnership between Monty Tech and Leominster High School had become a recurring program that continued to flourish. She left behind a legacy that ensured no future first-year student would have to worry about whether they could pursue music at a trade school. The project touched the lives of students in two communities, fostering a sense of unity that bridged gaps between educational approaches. Kelsey had proven that one girl's vision could change the cultural fabric of her school forever.

The growth Kelsey experienced as a leader prepared her for a future that was both global and deeply personal. As she moved on to college in Pennsylvania to study either business or early childhood education, she carried the confidence of someone who had managed international-level logistics. She also expanded her outreach through a YouTube channel, where she shared uplifting Christian videos and songs to impact a generation from one end of the sea to the other. She received feedback from people in different countries who were moved by her words and positivity, proving that her voice could reach far beyond Massachusetts.

Kelsey's journey is a reminder that the world is full of potential waiting for a leader to start the song. Her project was like a tuning fork—a single clear note that helped two different schools find their common rhythm. Kelsey crafted a mission that provided warmth and harmony to hundreds of students. She is a reminder that when we are brave enough to connect our communities, we create a symphony of hope that will be heard for generations to come.

Kelsey Aggrey discovered that leadership is like learning a new piece of music: it begins with a few uncertain notes, requires hours of practice through the difficult passages, and eventually blossoms into a performance that moves everyone who hears it. Her project didn't just build a band; it built a sound bridge that allowed two different schools to cross into a shared world of creativity. Kelsey took the broken silence of her school and used the heat of her passion to fuse it into a solid legacy of unity. She is a reminder that the most beautiful music we ever make is the kind that brings people together to sing the same song of possibility.

Chapter 8
Pantry Professor

Anushka Rawat (Ep 103)

Mystery Of Peanut Butter And Pasta

Anushka Rawat's journey toward making a massive impact on her community didn't start in high school; it began when she was just six years old. While most first graders were busy playing with blocks or learning to ride bikes, Anushka was walking through the doors of the Gateway 180 homeless shelter to volunteer. Because she spent so many years helping there, she started to notice something that most people overlooked. She saw families leaving food pantries with bags filled with a random assortment of items—things like jars of peanut butter, boxes of pasta, and cans of vegetables. To anyone else, it just looked like groceries, but Anushka saw the confusion on the faces of the people receiving them.

She realized that when you get a mix of ingredients that don't seem to go together, it is incredibly hard to turn them into an actual meal. If you have pasta but no sauce, or peanut butter but no bread, what do you do? Anushka watched as people struggled to utilize the food they were given, and she knew there had to be a better way to help them. She didn't want the food to sit on a shelf simply because someone didn't know a recipe; she wanted to give them the tools to create something delicious and nutritious for their families. This deep, personal connection to the shelter was the spark for her project.

Anushka decided she would create a professional cookbook specifically designed for the ingredients found in food pantries. She was passionate about this because she knew the people she was trying to help. She had been volunteering with them for years, and that passion kept her going even when the work became difficult. She wasn't just doing a school assignment; she was trying to solve a real-world problem for her neighbors. She knew that if she could teach people how to cook with what they had, she could help reduce food insecurity in a way that truly lasted.

Testing Sixty Flavors

Anushka knew that if she wanted people to use her cookbook, the recipes had to be more than just okay—they had to be great. She started by doing extensive research, reaching out to almost every food pantry in the Missouri region to ask exactly what they gave to their clients. She took all those lists and identified the common ingredients to create a master list that would serve as the foundation for her book. Every single recipe she wrote had to stick strictly to those ingredients to ensure that anyone using the book could make the meals.

Creating the recipes was a huge job. Anushka spent months scouring the internet for ideas, then adapting them to fit her pantry-staple list. If a recipe called for a fancy vegetable that wasn't in the pantry, she figured out a substitution that worked just as well. But she didn't just trust her own taste buds. She built a massive team of tasters to make sure every dish was a winner. She recruited her peers, her school friends, and even her dad's coworkers to help her test over 60 different recipes. It was a community effort, with everyone contributing a few recipes to cook and review, so no one person was overwhelmed.

To carry out this enormous task, Anushka followed a very organized set of steps:

- **Surveyed** dozens of local food pantries to create a master list of frequently distributed ingredients.
- **Developed** and edited over sixty unique recipes that use only items from that master list.
- **Recruited** a diverse team of friends and community volunteers to test and review each meal for taste and ease of use.
- **Formatted** the final book with clear wording and images to make it look professional.

The editing process turned out to be the longest and most difficult part of the execution. Anushka wanted the book to be uniform and look like something you would buy in a store. She had to align every picture, check every measurement, and make sure the wording was perfect for all 60 recipes. It was a lot of hard work for a high school freshman, but seeing the book finally come together made all those hours in the kitchen and at the computer worth it.

Wall Of Silence

Even though Anushka had a beautiful, finished product, her biggest challenge was just beginning. When she started reaching out to food pantries to see if they would distribute her cookbook, she was met with a wall of silence. She realized that to the pantry directors, she was just a high schooler asking them to hand out a random book, and many were worried about liability or their own internal policies. Some simply never responded, while others told her it was against their rules to distribute materials from outside organizations.

Anushka also ran into another major roadblock: nutrition guidelines. Every food pantry had its own set of rules about the kinds of health information it could share with its clients. Some pantries had very strict sodium limits or specific calorie requirements, and they couldn't give out Anushka's book unless every single recipe met those guidelines. She had to go back to her finished work and alter her recipes, changing the amounts of certain ingredients just to make sure she wasn't using too much salt or sugar. It was frustrating to have to redo work she thought was finished, but she knew she had to combat this problem if she wanted her book to reach the people who needed it.

To overcome the silence, Anushka had to get creative with her marketing. She realized that people needed to see the results before they would trust her. She coded a professional website, created eye-catching flyers, and started using word of mouth to spread the news. The real turning point came when she began hosting live cooking demonstrations. She went to the pantries and showed the staff and the clients exactly how easy and tasty the recipes were. Once people saw her in action and tasted the food, they were much more willing to say yes. Soon, word spread from one pantry to another, and organizations began reaching out to her to request copies.

Global Ripple Effect

What started as a goal to help five or six local pantries quickly exploded into something much bigger than Anushka ever imagined. By the time her project was complete, 192 food pantries across the Missouri and Illinois region had received her cookbook. She had connected with volunteers, staff members, and families from all walks of life, gaining a deeper understanding of her community that she never could have gotten from a textbook.

The impact was measurable and massive, but Anushka wasn't finished yet.

Her passion for the cause led her to transform her work into a 501 (c) (3) nonprofit organization called Young Chefs STL. She shifted the focus of her nonprofit to using accessible ingredients because she knew that fun cooking events don't help in the long term if people can't recreate the meals at home. Because of the wide reach of her organization, people from all over the world started contacting her to ask how they could get involved. Anushka was amazed to see her idea spark a global movement.

Today, Young Chefs STL has chapters and cookbook initiatives in places as far away as Canada and India. Anushka has learned so much about different cultures through these international connections. For example, her partners in India are making their own versions of the cookbook, altering the recipes to fit the ingredients available in their local pantries, which are very different from those in the United States. Anushka noted that in India, the book's ethnic food section features American dishes, while the main recipes are traditional Indian. She loves seeing how people are using her idea to help others connect with their roots, using whatever diverse ingredients they have on hand.

Coding A Future

Looking back on her journey, Anushka realized that she had learned the most important lesson of all: she can do big things. Starting such a massive project as a freshman was intimidating, and there were times when she felt stuck or discouraged. She admitted there was even a four-month period during her sophomore year where she didn't do any work at all because she was so overwhelmed. But she stayed resilient, leaning on her mentor, Sandy, and her family to keep pushing forward. She learned that if she set her mind to something, she could provide results that changed lives.

Anushka's growth as a leader extended into STEM as well. She has been part of a robotics team since the eighth grade, where she learned how to build robots, code websites, and conduct community outreach. Whether she is volunteering at an assisted living home with her robotics team or leading a nonprofit, Anushka is always looking for ways to give back to the community that supported her.

As she heads off to college, Anushka plans to study environmental studies and public policy, with the goal of eventually attending law school. She wants to become an environmental policy maker so she can tackle food insecurity from a different angle. She hopes to create laws that incentivize restaurants and grocery stores to donate their excess food waste to pantries rather than throwing it away. Her advice to any girl starting her own journey is simple: pick something you are truly passionate about and never be afraid to ask for help.

Anushka's story is like the master list she created for her cookbook—a collection of simple, everyday ingredients that, when mixed with enough passion and hard work, create something that nourishes an entire community. Just as she had to substitute ingredients to make a recipe work, she learned to adapt her plans when faced with silent inboxes and strict rules. Her nonprofit is the final, perfectly formatted page of a story that began with a first grader at a homeless shelter and grew into a global movement. Now, as she prepares to write the next chapter of her life in law and policy, she serves as a reminder that when you combine a girl's vision with the courage to lead, you can cook up a future where no one is left hungry, and every voice is heard.

Chapter 9
Verse of Belonging

Cydney Brown (Ep 84)

Rhythms Of Philadelphia

For Cydney Brown, the city of Philadelphia was more than just a place on a map; it was a living, breathing symphony of voices, history, and art. Growing up in the city of brotherly love, she found her own voice not through sports or traditional hobbies, but through the cadence of the spoken word. Poetry was her sanctuary, a way to process the world and reflect the vibrant culture of her community to itself. Her talent was undeniable, and she was eventually named the Youth Poet Laureate of Philadelphia. This prestigious title transformed her into a literal representative of the city's literary soul. This experience taught her that words have a unique power to bridge gaps and create a sense of place, but it also made her realize that many of her peers felt they didn't have a platform to share their own verses.

As a girl involved in community service for years, Cydney knew her Gold Award needed to reflect this passion. She didn't want just to write a poem; she wanted to build a community. Her personal motivation stemmed from the belief that literature and creative expression should be accessible to everyone, especially young girls navigating the complexities of high school life. She had seen how isolating the school environment could be when someone overlooks another's perspective. Being a representative of Philadelphia meant more than just attending ceremonies; it meant using her influence to create a space where other girls could feel as empowered by their voices as she felt by hers.

This background as a poet provided the perfect foundation for her mission. She understood the taboo that sometimes surrounded poetry—that it was too difficult, too formal, or not for everyone. She wanted to shatter that image and show that poetry was a tool for connection, a way to say, "I am here" and "I belong." With her notebook in hand and a vision for a more inclusive school culture, Cydney prepared to launch a project that would intertwine the art of the stanza with the heart of her community. She was ready to move from being a solo performer to a mentor who could help others find their own internal rhythm.

Stanza For The Silenced

When Cydney began the planning phase of her project, she knew she had to identify a specific group of girls who would benefit most from a literary program. She didn't want to host just a one-time event; she wanted to create a lasting program at her school that would foster long-term relationships and inclusion. She spent months researching how to structure a workshop that was both engaging and educational. She realized that for a program to be successful, it couldn't feel like another class with a teacher at the front of the room. It had to be a peer-to-peer experience where everyone felt like a shareholder in the creative process.

The identifying process for her participants was a lesson in community outreach. Cydney reached out to her peers and school administrators to find girls who were interested in writing, but who might feel intimidated by the larger school culture. She wanted to reach those who weren't part of the typical social groups—the girls who had stories to tell but didn't know where to put them. By focusing on a specific group within her high school, she was able to tailor her curriculum to their unique needs. She wanted to provide a safe space where they could explore their identities through verse without the fear of judgment that often exists in high school hallways.

Her goal was to foster a sense of belonging and self-worth through a literary program. She envisioned a space filled with the scratching of pens and the quiet confidence of shared secrets. Cydney's motivation wasn't just about the art; it was about the leadership growth she knew would happen when girls had the tools to advocate for themselves. She believed that if a girl could master a metaphor, she could master the confidence to speak up in a boardroom or a classroom. This mindset of empowerment through education became the heartbeat of her mission to connect her community one line at a time.

Building The Boundless Book

Executing a project of this scale required Cydney to become more than just a poet; she had to be a project manager, an organizer, and a publisher. The how of her project was a multifaceted journey that ranged from brainstorming individual poems to the physical creation of a collective work. She knew that to make her impact visible and measurable, she needed a tangible result the girls could hold in their hands, which led her to the ambitious goal of compiling and publishing a book featuring the participants' work in her program.

The actual implementation of the project was a cycle of creativity and logistics. Cydney had to manage her own academic workload while also serving as the primary mentor for her group. To ensure the mission was a success and that every girl's voice was represented with professional quality, she followed a very specific action plan:

- **Curriculum Development:** She designed a series of workshops that focused on different poetic forms and themes of identity, ensuring the activities were accessible to all skill levels.
- **Literary Mentorship:** Cydney led weekly sessions, offering feedback and encouragement to participants and helping them refine their verses for publication.

- **Professional Publishing:** She managed the technical process of compiling the poems into a book format, researching self-publishing tools and formatting requirements to ensure a high-quality finished product.
- **Community Distribution:** She organized an event to showcase the book, providing a platform for the girls to read their work aloud to an audience of families and school officials.

This phase of the project taught Cydney that leadership is as much about editing and organization as it is about the lightbulb moments of inspiration. She spent hours looking over drafts and making sure every page was perfect. She was no longer just a teenager with a hobby; she was a published author and program director overseeing a team of young writers. The book wasn't just a collection of paper; it was a blueprint for a more connected community. By the time the first copies arrived, Cydney had proven that one girl's vision could create a permanent record of achievement for dozens of others.

Rhyming Through Resistance

Even for a Poet Laureate, the road to a successful project was not without its detours and obstacles. Cydney faced significant external challenges when collaborating with her school. While the administration was supportive of the idea, navigating the red tape of school schedules and room availability proved to be a constant struggle. She often had to play phone tag with officials to secure space for her workshops. There were moments when the logistics felt like they were spinning out or when communication from the school slowed to a crawl. Cydney had to learn the value of persistence and how to send professional emails that got results.

Beyond the logistical hurdles, Cydney also faced the daunting task of publishing a book. She realized that the world of publishing is complex and filled with what-ifs. She had to research copyright laws, ISBNs, and the ins and outs of digital distribution. There were times when the technical side of the project felt overwhelming, especially for someone whose primary love was the creative side of writing. She admitted that accepting criticism from her own project mentors was a learning process. She had to learn that when someone suggested a change to her program book, it wasn't a rejection of her heart, but a way to make the final product even better.

The internal growth Cydney experienced during these trials was immense. She learned to roll with the punches and remain a steady leader even when things didn't go according to plan. She realized that being a leader meant staying in the room to figure things out when everyone else was ready to leave. She turned her fear of rejection into a source of self-confidence, realizing that her voice carried weight even in professional meetings with adults who had worked in literature for twenty years. Her journey through the resistance proved that a girl with enough determination can find a rhyme for even the most difficult problem.

Masterpiece In Progress

The impact of Cydney's project was both immediate and life-changing. One of her most special memories was watching the girls in her program stand up and read their poems for the very first time. She saw the visible difference in their posture and the cheek-to-cheek smiles that appeared when they realized people were listening to them. She had successfully promoted self-expression and created a safe space for her peers to be their authentic selves. The book they created together stands as a permanent resource in her school's library, ensuring that the project's legacy will continue to inspire first-year students for years after Cydney has moved on.

As she reached the goal line of her project, Cydney reflected on how far she had come since she first picked up a pen. She realized that she could do amazing things and that her work as a poet and a leader was just beginning. Her leadership growth had prepared her for the next big chapter of her life: attending Northwestern University. She plans to continue her studies in literature and

communications, carrying the skills she gained—
the professional development, the public speaking,
and the ability to pivot—into her college career.
She remains a girl at heart, committed to using her
voice to impact a generation and empower others
to tell their own stories.

Cydney's advice to other girls considering their own
major mission is not to fear the work. The journey
will have its ups and downs, but she believes the
outcome of seeing a project through to the finish is
worth every hour of work. She has transformed
from a quiet poet in Philadelphia into a global
advocate for literary inclusion. Cydney Brown is a
reminder that when we dare to write our own
future, we create a ripple effect that connects our
entire community, transforming a single stanza into
a symphony of hope.

Cydney discovered that leadership is like writing a
long poem: it requires a clear vision, a lot of
drafting, and the strength to share it with the world
eventually. Her project was more than just a book
or a workshop; it bridged the silence among girls at
her school, forging a community of writers. Just as
a poet carefully selects each word to ensure the
perfect rhythm, Cydney worked with precision and
heart to ensure her mission provided a solid
foundation for the next generation. She is a
reminder that the most durable things we build are
not made of stone or steel, but of the connections
we make when we decide to stand up and say that
every girl's story is a masterpiece in progress.

Chapter 10
Keepers Of Courage

Erica Dunne (Ep 52)

Cookie Trail To Discovery

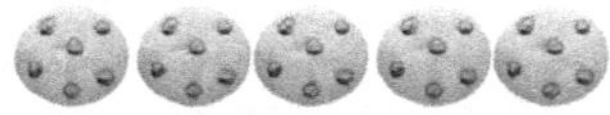

Erica Dunne's journey into the heart of her community began when she was only five years old. Every Veterans Day, she and her friends would bundle up against the crisp November air, clutching boxes of cookies to deliver to local heroes. For years, this was a simple tradition of gratitude. However, as Erica grew older, she noticed a touching pattern. The veterans weren't just waiting for a snack; they were waiting for a connection. Many of them would be standing by their doors, eager for the arrival of the local youth. When Erica stepped inside, she wasn't just entering a house; she was stepping into a living archive. These men and women would pull out dusty scrapbooks, faded newspaper clippings, and shiny service badges they had tucked away for decades.

As they shared their stories, Erica realized she was hearing history that was not written in any school textbook. She heard about moments of intense bravery, the quiet fear of the unknown, and the deep friendships formed in the face of conflict. But beneath the excitement of the stories, there was a heartbreaking realization. Many veterans admitted that, aside from their very closest family members, almost no one had ever asked them about their service. Erica saw these precious memories as fragile threads about to be lost forever. She felt a deep personal motivation to ensure these voices were captured and shared with the rest of the world.

The vision wasn't just about a one-time thank you anymore. Erica wanted to create a permanent community resource that would bridge the gap between the generations. She knew that as these veterans grew older, their stories became less accessible. As a dedicated Girl Scout who had spent over a decade in the program, she understood that leadership meant taking action when she saw a need. She decided to focus her Gold Award on preserving these unspoken accounts of courage. Her mission was to turn those private conversations by the front door into a legacy that her entire town could cherish. She was ready to move beyond simply delivering cookies and start delivering the truth of her neighbors' lives to the next generation.

Mapping The Memories

When Erica sat down to plan the structure of her mission, she knew she had to think like both a historian and a storyteller. She wanted her project to be more than just a list of names and dates; it needed to be an immersive experience. After much thought, she decided on a two-part approach. First, she would write and design a physical book. She believed that a book would be more accessible than a simple website because it would allow readers to physically flip through history, seeing the progression of service members chronologically from World War II to the modern conflicts in Afghanistan and Iraq. She wanted to include maps and high-quality photos so that people could visualize exactly where these heroes had served.

However, Erica also recognized that technology could offer something a printed page never could: the sound of a human voice. She decided to build a companion website to host the audio recordings of her interviews. She knew that hearing the emotion, the pauses, and the strength in a veteran's voice would provide a more in-depth research experience for anyone using the resource. An ambitious undertaking for a high school student, Erica realized she couldn't do it alone. She reached out to her local historical society, the Newcastle Historical Society, which became an invaluable partner in her journey.

The historical society provided more than just encouragement; they gave Erica a professional framework for her work. They introduced her to the Library of Congress method of conducting veteran interviews. This standard ensured that she wasn't just chatting; she was collecting vital data like rank, branch, and title, while also securing the proper legal release forms to share the stories publicly. Erica had to learn the importance of meticulous documentation. She spent her summer coordinating meetings, checking her recording equipment, and mapping out a timeline to interview

18 veterans. She was no longer just a student with a hobby; she was a professional archivist building a bridge of memory for her community.

Turning Tapes Into Truth

The actual execution of the project was where the hard work truly began. Erica spent hundreds of hours listening to her interview tapes and transcribing every word to ensure accuracy. But as she looked at the growing piles of transcripts, she realized that dry reports wouldn't capture the spirit of the people she had met. She didn't want each chapter to start with a date and a location. She wanted to write compelling non-fiction that made readers feel they were sitting right there with the veteran. This intent required her to analyze each conversation to find the crucial thing the veteran said or a specific, vivid experience that could serve as a powerful opening for their story.

Erica stepped into the role of a project manager and fundraiser to handle the complex needs of her book production. She faced a significant challenge when she realized the cost of high-quality printing. She refused to short-change the veterans by using cheap paper or black-and-white photos; she wanted glossy pages and full-color images of the badges and clippings they had shown her, which meant she had to become a business leader to fund her vision.

To ensure the book reached the professional standards the veterans deserved, Erica took several strategic actions:

- **Fundraised** through multiple community bake sales and pre-sold copies of the book to neighbors and local organizations to cover the high printing costs.
- **Collaborated** with a board member from the historical society to plan and organize her town's very first official Veterans Day celebration.
- **Transcribed** hours of audio tapes into written format while meticulously verifying dates and locations of service to ensure total historical accuracy.
- **Implemented** the Library of Congress standards for every interview to ensure the stories were preserved in a format recognized by national archives.

The writing process pushed Erica to grow in ways she hadn't expected. She had always loved writing fiction, but this project forced her to master the art of details and primary source material. She learned that a leader must be persistent even when the work feels long and tedious. Between the bake sales and the late-night editing sessions, she remained focused on the goal. She knew that every cookie she sold and every sentence she polished brought her one step closer to honoring the people who had given so much for their country. By the time the book was ready for the printer, Erica had proven that she had the grit to see a massive vision through to completion.

Classroom Connection

One of the most rewarding parts of Erica's mission was seeing her project come to life for the youngest members of her community. She didn't just want the book to sit on a shelf in the historical society; she wanted it to spark a conversation. She designed an interactive program specifically for elementary school students to teach them about the origins of Veterans Day and Memorial Day. Initially, she was nervous about how to make these distant issues feel relevant to seven and eight-year-olds who might not have any service members in their own families. She decided to use high-energy games and storytelling to pull them into the history.

The magic happened when she held up a photo of one of the veterans from her book. A student's eyes went wide, and they shouted, "Oh, that's my neighbor! I didn't know he was a veteran!", the full circle moment Erica had hoped for. It reminded the children—and the adults in the room—that veterans aren't just figures from the past; they are our doctors, our teachers, and the people living right next door. By putting a face and a local story to the word veteran, Erica made history feel personal. She was successfully connecting the different pockets of her community, showing that everyone has a story worth hearing.

Erica also organized her town's first Veterans Day celebration, which included a panel where veterans spoke directly to the public. Even when a global pandemic forced her to rethink her plans, she remained dedicated. She adapted the event to be socially distanced, ensuring the community could still honor its heroes safely. Seeing her town come together to listen and say thank you was the visible proof of the impact she had made. She had taken a passion and used it to strengthen her community's bonds. She has proven that when you provide a platform for truth, people will show up to listen.

Legacy Of Listening

Reflecting on her journey, Erica realized that the project had fundamentally changed how she viewed herself and her future. She went from a quiet writer of fictional stories to a confident public speaker who addresses town boards and high-ranking West Point officials. She learned that if you know your topic well and do your research, you can handle any interview or presentation with grace. Her earlier experiences, such as helping her troop propose a National Thank You First Responders Day, laid the foundation for the leadership she demonstrated during her project. She realized that the skills she built—attention to detail, professional communication, and project management—were tools she would carry with her for the rest of her life.

Erica's impact continues to grow, even after she received her Gold Award. She used her interviews as the basis for a semester-long research paper at school, showing how community service can blend perfectly with academic life. But her dreams go far beyond her own graduation. She is determined to take her mission to the national stage. She hopes to create a national organization that provides funding and resources to help others—both girls in the program and those outside it—interview veterans in their own communities. She wants to ensure that the distinguished stories of the past are not silenced by the passage of time.

Erica's story is a powerful reminder that history is not just a collection of dates on a timeline, but a tapestry of individual lives woven together with care. Just as a single thread might seem small, when combined with others, it creates a story strong enough to withstand the tests of time. By opening her heart and a book, Erica showed her community that the greatest way to honor the past is to listen to the present, ensuring that every hero has a seat at the table of our collective memory. Her project was the spark that turned a quiet neighborhood into a connected community, all dedicated to guarding the courage of those who served.

Chapter 11
Career Catalyst

Julie Mandimutsira (Ep 81)

Shadow In The Food Bank

Julie Mandimutsira was a girl who understood the value of hard work, but she often felt like she was swimming against a tide of confusion when it came to her own future. For thirteen years, she had been taught to see a need and fill it, yet she found that even the best intentions could sometimes go astray. Her journey toward her Gold Award began with a frustrating sight at a place she loved: the Second Mile Mission food bank in her hometown. Julie was a frequent volunteer there, helping to pack crates of food that would eventually reach families in desperate need. During one of her sessions, she noticed something that deeply saddened her. Two volunteers, roughly her own age, had strategically positioned themselves behind stacks of crates, hiding in the shadows to avoid doing any actual work.

It was clear to Julie that they weren't there because they cared about the mission; they were simply trying to clock in so they could get their required volunteer hours without lifting a finger. This volunteer disengagement wasn't just a minor annoyance; it directly impacted the food bank's ability to serve its clients. Julie began to wonder why these teens felt so unmotivated. She realized that they likely viewed service as a boring chore rather than an opportunity. At the same time, Julie was grappling with her own internal stress. As she entered the spring of her senior year of high school, she still wasn't entirely sure what she wanted to do with her life or what her college major should be.

She realized that many of her peers shared this insecurity. In high school, it is difficult to find hands-on experiences in career fields like engineering, marketing, or counseling because most companies aren't looking to hire teenagers. Julie had a lightbulb moment: what if she could solve both problems at once? If she could connect students with volunteer organizations that matched their specific career interests, service would no longer feel like a burden. Instead, it would become a way for teens to try on a career while providing vital help to the community. This personal motivation became the foundation for her project, which aimed to bridge the gap between youth volunteers and the organizations that desperately needed their energy and passion.

Blueprint For Professional Service

Turning an ambitious idea into a reality required Julie to think like a professional coordinator. She didn't want just to hold a one-time event; she wanted to create a system that allowed participants to explore their potential. Julie envisioned a series of virtual volunteer fairs where organizations could pitch their missions to interested students, much like a job fair. She knew that she couldn't build this bridge alone, so she began searching for the right partners to scale her project. Her most beneficial connection was with the college and career readiness counselor at her high school. This mentor was instrumental in Julie's success, providing the professional guidance needed to reach students across the entire school district.

Julie spent months researching organizations, looking for those that offered diverse opportunities in fields such as education, technology, and project management. She didn't just want food banks on the list; she wanted a boon of good ideas that would appeal to every type of student. Her planning was meticulous, involving dozens of meetings and the development of professional marketing materials.

Julie transformed from a student into a project manager. To keep her mission moving forward, she and her team followed a specific set of implementation steps:

- She **collaborated** with her school district's leadership to ensure that flyers and informational packets reached nearly a hundred interested students.
- She **organized** and hosted a series of virtual fairs that successfully highlighted 35 unique

> volunteer-driven organizations to her community.

- She **launched** a dedicated website as a permanent resource for students to continue accessing the fair's recordings and find new service opportunities.
- She **recruited** participants for youth development programs, such as Operation Get to Work, to help middle schoolers begin their career exploration early.

This stage of the project taught Julie that leadership is about more than just having a vision; it's about the logistics of communication. When she sent her flyers to the counselor, she saw immediate results: 86 participants signed up to hear more about the organization. She was no longer just a girl who saw a problem at a food bank; she was a leader who was actively creating a pathway for her peers to find their own sense of purpose. By providing these connections, she was ensuring that the next generation of volunteers would be engaged, eager, and ready to make a real difference in the world.

Mountain Of Self-Doubt

? ? ? ? ?

Despite her clear plan and strong partnerships, Julie hit a major roadblock that she hadn't anticipated: her own internal struggle. As a girl who was balancing a rigorous high school schedule with numerous extracurricular activities, she found herself falling into a pattern of procrastination. It took her nearly two years to complete her project, starting in the spring of 2018 and not reaching the finish line until the winter of 2020, just days before the official deadline. At the time, she told herself she was simply too busy, but looking back with hindsight being 2020, she realized the truth was much deeper.

Underneath the excuses of being a busy senior, Julie was struggling with significant doubts and insecurities. She often wondered if her project was good enough or if anyone would even care about the virtual fairs she was working so hard to create. She feared that the council or the community might reject something she loved and had invested so much of herself into. This fear of failure weighed her down, slowing her progress and making the tedious paperwork feel like a mountain to climb.

What ultimately helped Julie push past herself was her team's unwavering support. Her parents, her project advisor, and her mentor refused to let her give up on her vision. They were committed to pushing her past her doubts and providing the guidance she needed whenever she felt stuck in the lulls of the process. Julie learned that a leader is not someone who never feels afraid, but someone who listens to the voices of the people who encourage them. She realized that it's "okay to reach out to people and ask others for help because you're not the only person in this project".

This period of her life was a masterclass in perseverance, teaching her that even the largest goals are achievable if you are willing to take things one day at a time and face your fears.

Spark Of Connection

When the virtual volunteer fairs finally went live, the impact was immediate and wonderful. Julie watched as her months of planning turned into real-life connections between students and community leaders. One of her favorite stories from the fair featured a student passionate about sports but unsure how to turn that passion into community service. Julie was able to put him in direct contact with the program leader for a youth sports organization that needed coaches and referees. Seeing that specific successful connection happen right before her eyes made all the long nights of website design feel worth the effort.

The fairs highlighted 35 unique organizations, offering students a wide range of career-aligned roles they never would have found on their own. The community's feedback was glowing, and Julie was featured in the newspaper for her alma mater, an experience she described as wonderful. She realized that by giving students a choice in how they served, she was transforming the community's view of youth volunteers. They were no longer the teens hiding behind crates; they were future biomedical engineers, educators, and marketers invested in the missions they supported.

Through this process, Julie's own confidence began to soar. She realized she could impact the world in a way that would create real, lasting change. She had taken on a global issue, such as volunteer disengagement. She addressed it at a local level, proving that one girl with a computer and a mission can rewrite the narrative for her entire community. The project wasn't just about the number of attendees; it was about the quality of the engagement and the permanent resources she left on her website. Julie had successfully built a bridge of belonging, ensuring that service would be a tool for self-discovery for years to come.

Navigating New Horizons

Julie's willingness to explore the unknown shaped her leadership. Before finishing her project, she participated in a life-changing destination trip to Panama and Costa Rica for a scuba and sea turtle adventure. Traveling internationally without her parents was crazy and initially scary, but it taught her about independence and allowed her to mature quite a bit. She spent two weeks releasing baby sea turtles into the ocean and earning her scuba-diving certification, experiences she credits with helping her figure out who she wanted to be as a young woman. These adventures gave her the most fulfilling emotion of her life, fueling her desire to continue serving the community in her young adulthood.

Today, Julie is a student at Duke University, pursuing a degree in biomedical engineering. She chose Duke because of the number of opportunities and clubs available on its beautiful campus. Her time in the program taught her that the skills she used for her project—collaborating with experts, troubleshooting technical issues, and managing complex timelines—are the same skills she uses every day as an engineer. She is currently interested in specializing in immunoengineering or virtual reality engineering, always looking for the next way to use technology to help others.

Julie's story reminds us that a community is like a vast ocean, and finding your place in it can sometimes feel like diving into the deep without a map. If you dare to build your own bridge and have the persistence to keep swimming through the shadows of doubt, you will eventually find a horizon where your passions and your purpose meet. Julie didn't just host a few fairs; she created a compass for her community, proving that when a girl decides to lead, she can help everyone around her find the right path to a brighter, more engaged future. Her final words of encouragement to any girl starting her own journey are simple: "Go for it. Your ideas are worth it".

Chapter 12
Purrfect Home

Gabrielle Ontiveros (Ep 161)

Stray in the Kayaks

Gabrielle, known to her friends as Gabby, grew up with a deep love for animals that started right in her own backyard in Lake City, Florida. Her story began when a mysterious visitor appeared near her house—a stray cat that seemed to have no home to call its own. This cat didn't just wander by; she decided to make Gabby's yard her sanctuary. Time after time, the cat sought shelter in the family's kayaks to give birth to her kittens. Gabby watched as this small, independent creature struggled to find safety and comfort in the world. It was a sight that pulled at her heartstrings, but she wasn't sure what to do until a neighbor named Mary stepped in to help. Mary was a kind woman who knew exactly how to handle the situation. She helped Gabby trap the cats and take them to a special place called Operation Catnip, a local clinic that specialized in caring for community cats.

Through this experience, Gabby learned that there was a big difference between a regular pet and a community cat. While a pet lives inside with a family, community cats live outdoors and are often cared for by many people in a neighborhood rather than just one. These cats aren't necessarily wild or feral; many are quite social and happy to see their human neighbors, especially if those neighbors provide a steady supply of food. Gabby learned that these cats help the environment by controlling pests and rodents, but they need help staying healthy and preventing their population from growing too large. Maintaining the population is where the trap-neuter-release (TNR) process comes in, neutering cats so they don't continue reproducing in ways that could be invasive to the environment.

Gabby's bond with the cat that lived in her kayaks was the spark that ignited a much bigger fire. She realized that while she loved her own cat, there were thousands of other community cats in the Gainesville area that needed advocates. She saw that the people working at local shelters were under a lot of stress, and she wanted to find a way to help relieve that pressure. Her personal motivation was simple: she loved cats, and she wanted to benefit a community that had already begun to feel like home. She decided that her project would focus on providing these animals with the one thing every creature deserves—a safe place to sleep.

Rejection and Redirection

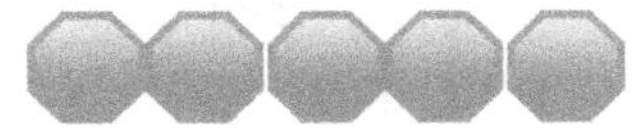

Before Gabby could start building her purrfect homes, she hit a major roadblock that many people face when starting a big project. She originally had a very different idea, much more ambitious than caring for cats. Her first proposal focused on serious topics like drug use and relationship abuse among teenagers. She wanted to conduct deep research and run a massive awareness campaign with endless resources. However, the committee that reviews these projects told her no. They felt the idea was too big for one teenager to handle while still in high school, especially given the complex ethical issues involved in such a sensitive topic. Gabby was incredibly upset at first. She felt like her great idea had been thrown away, and she struggled to understand why she was told to scale it down.

While it was a difficult time for Gabby, she had a strong support system to help her through the frustration. Her troop leader and her mother, who was the co-leader, refused to let her give up. They had been with her for over ten years and knew she had the strength to finish what she started. Her troop leader sat her down and pointed out a simple truth: Gabby loved cats. Why not focus on a cause that was fun and aligned with her interests? Gabby realized she didn't have to do something crazy or different just to reach a milestone; she could do something she was passionate about, which would make the work feel like no work at all. She learned to embrace a quote that would stick with her for years: "Rejection is a redirection".

Even after she switched her focus to cats, the path wasn't perfectly smooth. She faced three rejections of her proposals before finally getting the green light to move forward. Each time her proposal was sent back, she had to practice a skill that is very hard for middle schoolers and high schoolers alike: overcoming rejection. She realized that these experiences were building bricks for her future. They were teaching her how to handle applications and hurdles she would eventually face in the professional world. By the time her proposal was accepted, Gabby was more resilient and more focused than ever before. She was ready to take on the Gainesville heat and start building.

Building a Blueprint

Building high-quality homes for outdoor cats was a task that required a lot of math, a lot of sweat, and a lot of help from the community. Gabby didn't want just to use simple styrofoam bins; she wanted to create structures that were durable and would truly protect the cats from the unpredictable Florida weather. She had to figure out a design that would keep water out while still being comfortable for the cats. Her research involved navigating unique variables, such as finding the right angles for the wood and ensuring the materials could withstand the intense humidity and heat of the Florida summer.

Because she didn't have all the materials she needed at home, Gabby had to become a fundraiser and a communicator. She walked into local businesses and asked for help. She was pleasantly surprised when the Home Depot staff were "so sweet" and gave her a $50 credit to buy the supplies she needed. She also worked closely with her father, a handyman who helped her determine the best way to assemble the storage bins and the wood into a high-quality structure. Working in the heat was frustrating and exhausting, but Gabby stayed locked in on her goal.

The execution of her plan was about more than just construction; it was about creating a sustainable system for the cats. To carry out her project, she took the following actions:

- **Solicited** donations from local businesses and neighbors to secure storage bins and high-quality wood.
- **Engineered** a waterproof design that would provide shelter from the rain and shade from the extreme Florida sun.
- **Collaborated** with the staff at Operation Catnip to ensure the houses go to the locations that need them most.

By the time she finished, Gabby had built and deployed several cat houses that were a major upgrade from the basic shelters many community cats were used to. She had turned her backyard observations into a professional construction project that directly helped a local organization. The process of building these houses wasn't just about hammers and nails; it was about problem-solving and learning to work with the resources she had available to make a lasting impact.

Cats of the University

The next part of Gabby's project took her to the heart of the University of Florida campus. While many people see college students as busy adults focused only on their studies, Gabby noticed that the university's community cats were a major part of student life. In fact, one specific cat named Tenders had become a local celebrity. Gabby realized that these cats provided significant mental health benefits to the students, offering a sense of comfort and a reason to smile during stressful exam seasons. She wanted to raise awareness of these benefits and teach the student body how to care for their campus neighbors.

Gabby used social media to spread important messages about the local colonies. She highlighted specific cats, like Baby, a sassy, cutesy cat who lived near Pew Hall, to help students feel a personal connection to the animals. Through her posts, she educated her peers about the dangers of leaving food in open cans. She shared a sad story about Tenders, who had recently suffered a painful injury on her tongue because someone had left a sharp can lid on the ground. Gabby used this incident to teach people that while feeding the cats is helpful, cleaning up after yourself and using safe feeding methods are just as important for the animals' safety.

This phase of the project required Gabby to serve as a leader and educator. She volunteered at Operation Catnip, helping with daily tasks that keep the clinic running. She learned that if you want to help an organization, sometimes the best thing you can do is just send an email and ask, "Hey, do you need help?" Her willingness to put herself out there and volunteer on the ground enabled her to identify the root causes of the issues facing community cats. She saw that education and volunteer support were the two things the community needed most to keep the feline population healthy and safe.

New Kind of Mentor

By the time Gabby finished her project, she had changed. Completing such a big task during her last year of high school while transitioning to a new city was a massive undertaking. She had moved from Lake City to Gainesville, and the project helped her adjust to her new home. It forced her to be more social, put herself out there, and explore the city using public transit. She realized that "being alone is not what's meant for mankind" and that having a community of supporters is the key to getting hard things done.

Gabby's time in Girl Scouts, spanning over eleven years, had turned her into a mentor for younger girls. She looked at the younger members of her troop and realized that she had seen them grow up from babies into people with their own thoughts and ideas. She understood that she was now part of a wheel of mentorship that keeps the community strong. Her success showed other girls that even if you get rejected and even if things feel impossible, you can still build something from the ground up. She now proudly identifies herself as a leader within the Women's Student Association at her university, connecting with other girls who have also achieved high honors.

As Gabby looks toward her future, she plans to become a professor and researcher in psychology. She wants to study how teenagers and young adults grow and develop, a passion she discovered through her own years of mentorship and service. She encourages every girl to stay in Girl Scouts and finish their projects, even when the time commitment feels like a struggle. She believes that the skills she learned—like handling rejection, managing her time, and advocating for a cause— are things that will stay on her resume and in her heart forever.

Gabby's project required the patience of several proposals to turn her love for cats into a purrfect home for her community. Now, as she walks across her college campus, she doesn't just see a stray cat; she sees a neighbor that she helped protect. Her story serves as a reminder that when you take something you love and turn it into a cause, you aren't just building a cat house—you are building a future where every creature has a place to belong.

Chapter 13 Strengthening Communities

Observing Where Connections are Needed

As you conclude the narratives in this book, you have witnessed a masterclass in turning personal history into professional impact. You saw how a simple tradition of delivering cookies led a five-year-old girl to discover a living archive of history tucked away in the dusty scrapbooks and memories of local veterans. By moving beyond a one-time thank-you, she built a bridge of memory through a physical book and a digital archive, ensuring those fragile threads of memory were not lost. You read about a young woman who noticed a shadow in the food bank, where volunteer disengagement turned service into a chore rather than a career catalyst. Her action to match students with volunteer organizations based on their professional interests transformed teenagers from hiding behind crates into future leaders. You met a girl who saw a stray in the kayaks and realized that community cats provide mental health benefits to the neighbors who care for them. Even after multiple rejections, she engineered waterproof homes that served as sanctuaries for these silent neighbors.

In a world filled with digital fog and isolation, you encountered advocates who built bridges of sound and ink. One leader fine-tuned her signal by launching a podcast titled Thoughts for Your Thoughts, using audio education to help her peers look outside their inner bubble. Another turned a piece of paper and a stamp into a powerful connection, building a pen pal empire that spanned the ocean to a navy base in Japan. You saw how a pantry renovation could pulse through a community when a girl used her voice to build an ergonomic stand for a conveyor belt, respecting the rhythm of the older volunteers. Whether it was creating a book nook sanctuary for children escaping domestic violence or designing a craft group named Abilities with Possibilities to bridge the gap between neurotypical and neurodiverse minds, these leaders proved that one person can hold a community together. They navigated the mystery of peanut butter and pasta to create the global movement Young Chefs STL and launched a verse of belonging to give a platform to silenced voices in high school hallways. Their collective legacy serves as a blueprint for your own journey, reminding you that your voice has weight and your actions create ripples of awareness that reach far beyond your own backyard.

Drafting Your Own Mission

Transitioning from a reader to a leader means moving into the deep end of the implementation process and finding your own lightbulb moment. The stories you have read are not just inspirations; they are proof that the mechanics of making an impact—organizing a team, setting a timeline, and staying dedicated—are skills you can master. Before you dive into the toolkit, take a moment to reflect on the mirror of the past and recognize that your unique background is the foundation of your advocacy. You have seen that even a shy girl can transform into a confident representative of her community, literally carrying a banner of achievement through the streets. Now, it is your turn to step out of your comfort zone and into the world of policy, engineering, or community service.

This toolkit will guide you through the swamp of regulations and the techniques of professional communication. You will learn to focus on your goals even when the initial response is cold or when you face the waiting game of the approval process. Leadership requires you to be the person who holds the map when the road gets confusing, managing schedules and navigating the red tape of school boards and council committees. By following these steps, you will move from identifying a gap in understanding to creating a permanent shift in your community's culture.

Prepare to be the enabler of the change the world is waiting for, understanding that every huge achievement begins with a single, small decision to try. Your growth as a leader starts the moment you move from being a witness to being the architect of a better world.

Step One: Identify the Gap

Becoming a civic leader begins with identifying a problem you are truly passionate about, as this passion is the fuel that will keep you going when the hours get long and the deadlines get stressful. Use your personal history as a mirror to find your mission. Whether you are an animal lover, a coder, or someone who cares about social justice, your background is your greatest asset. You don't have to wait for someone else to fix a problem—you can be the voice for the voiceless. To find your focus, you must become a keen observer of your environment, looking for civic deserts or taboos that others might have overlooked.

- **Observe** Your Community: Look for gaps in services, safety, or inclusion. Ask yourself what bare necessities are missing in your local schools or parks.

- **Research** the Why: Investigate whether a lack of education, outdated laws, or a civic drought causes a problem.

- **Identify** Your Unique Angle: How can your specific talents—like art, robotics, or public speaking—be used to solve the issue?

Don't be discouraged if your small idea feels overwhelming at first, as leadership is a slow-burning flame nurtured by showing up year after year. You must be ready to knock loud enough to garner attention, even when doors seem closed. Every major project, from protecting child vloggers to building a portable racetrack, started with a single person deciding that a problem was worth solving. Find your inspiration and take that first step toward advocacy.

Step Two: Mechanics of Impact

Once your mission is clear, you must move into the planning phase, which is a masterclass in professional development. Turning a vision into reality requires you to become a project manager who can handle the logistics of construction, the red tape of liability, and the detail work of editing. You will need to build a team of shareholders and advisors—government officials, teachers, or experts—who can provide real-world insights. Your execution should follow a specific design loop to ensure high-quality impact.

- **Draft a Plan**: Create a sustainable program manual or curriculum that meets rigorous standards.

- **Build a Professional Presence**: Use digital marketing and graphic design to give your mission a distinct and beautiful brand.

- **Master the Art of the Pitch**: Practice delivering a thirty-second pitch and writing clear, professional emails to busy administrators.

- **Be Persistent with Follow-Ups**: Don't just send one email; send follow-ups, make phone calls, and ask for referrals.

- **Implement a Development Cycle**: Design, test, and improve your resources based on feedback and on what works and what doesn't.

As you navigate this stage, prepare for detours and obstacles, such as the high printing costs of a community book or the challenge of recruiting a team of volunteers for large-scale renovations. You must learn to pivot and adapt, much as you might rethink a local celebration during a pandemic or transform a small idea into a virtual volunteer fair when traditional paths are blocked. Being a leader requires the grit to remain persistent through tedious work and late-night sessions, even as you balance a rigorous school schedule with your mission. Your capacity to stay professional and steady while navigating red tape or sending professional emails to break through the lack of response from local organizations will ultimately set your masterpiece in progress apart from those that never reach the finish line.

Step Three: Becoming the Enabler of Change

The final measure of a successful mission is ensuring it lives on after you move on and that its impact reaches as far as possible. You have seen how projects can span 23 states and six countries through global links and digital maps. A true leader ensures their work is sustainable by passing the torch to someone else who can keep the flame alive. Ensuring your mission becomes a permanent shift in your community's culture rather than just a one-time event is vital.

- **Document and Measure**: Use data, surveys, and global impact maps to prove the effectiveness of your work.

- **Share Your Resources**: Distribute your toolkits and digital brochures so people in other places can repeat your mission.

- **Create a Permanent Hub**: Build a dedicated website or reference guide that serves as a lasting resource for others.

- **Mentor Your Successor**: Identify a younger person or organization in your school or community to lead the project after you.

By the time you submit your final report, you will have built a foundation for a life of impact and honor. The skills you gained—public speaking, managing complex teams, and navigating bureaucracies—will serve you in college, the military, or any professional career you choose. You might find yourself debating on a national stage or advising the CEO of a major organization. Remember, the best things are often the ones you've worked the hardest to create. Your project was the spark that lit a fire of advocacy, and now that fire will guide you as you bridge into your future, ready to lead the world.

Final Chord of Connection

♪♪♪♪♪♪♪♪♪♪♪♪♪♪♪

Your leadership journey is not just about finishing a project; it is about becoming the architect of a more connected world. Remember that every huge achievement begins with a single, small decision to try. Whether you are following a cookie trail to discovery or finding a symphony of unity between different communities, your willingness to bridge the gap between people is what transforms a neighborhood into a true community. When you encounter a wall of silence or the cloud of procrastination, look back at how far you have already come and simply take a moment to breathe. You have the power to turn a silent trade school into a musical sanctuary or a shadow in a food bank into a career catalyst for your peers. Trust that your ideas are worth it, and as you step into your own mission, know that your voice is the tuning fork that can start a harmony of change across the globe. Go for it, because the most lasting thing you will build is the connections you make when you decide to lead.

💛 Build unity with
with
your voice 💛

ABOUT THE AUTHOR

Sheryl M. Robinson is a podcaster, mentor, and speaker dedicated to helping teens and young adults discover their unique gifts, talents, and abilities, creating a path toward their dreams.

Sheryl holds a Master of Arts in Servant Leadership from Viterbo University and a Bachelor's in Accounting from Southern Illinois University – Carbondale. She has been a proud member of Girl Scouts for more than 30 years. Her passion for supporting teens — especially those pursuing the Girl Scout Gold Award — led her to create *Hearts of Gold*, a YouTube series and podcast featuring Gold Award Girl Scouts from across the world.

In recognition of her work elevating and supporting the Girl Scout Highest Awards, Sheryl has been honored with the GSUSA Thanks II Award, the organization's highest recognition for service.

Recognizing the need for younger Girl Scouts to have resources and role models as they pursue the Bronze Award and Silver Award, Sheryl created this middle-grade book series to share inspiring stories of leadership, courage, and community change.

She deeply believes that the Girl Scout Highest Awards not only make the world a better place but also transform the Girl Scouts who earn them — building lifelong changemakers, confident problem-solvers, and compassionate leaders.

ACKNOWLEDGMENTS

Creating this book has been a journey shaped by many remarkable people, and I am deeply grateful for each of you.

To **my mom, Jean**, who first started me in Girl Scouts many years ago and planted the seeds of everything that would follow.

To **my daughter, Nikki**, a Bronze, Silver, and Gold Award Girl Scout whose dedication inspires me every day. Watching you flourish through each phase of your life is one of my greatest joys.

To **my husband, Mark,** thank you for always supporting me and the many plates you quietly set beside me while I typed away. I thank God for bringing you into my life every day.

To **Kenzie,** thank you for reading the first draft and sharing thoughtful feedback. Your insights helped shape this book and made it stronger.

To **all the Gold Award Girl Scouts** who have shared their stories on the Hearts of Gold podcast — thank you for trusting me with your journeys. Your courage, creativity, and leadership inspire thousands.

To the **Girl Scout leaders, volunteers, and parents** who support these incredible young women: your encouragement makes meaningful change possible.

To **Cassie**, who encouraged me to restart my Girl Scout journey when my daughter joined Girl Scouts.

A heartfelt thank you to **Stacie and Shannan**, who have listened to me talk about this book for years and never stopped encouraging me to make it happen.

To **Walter**, my podcast editor for the first nine years, and **Tommy**, my new editor — and to their entire family, especially **Greg**, whose podcasting challenge a decade ago helped set all of this into motion.

And finally, to **Elsie, Rob, Cliff, Daniel, and Jessica** — thank you for your inspiration, for keeping the process fun, for sharing your knowledge, and for helping Hearts of Gold continue to grow.

This project exists because of each of you.
Thank you for helping bring these stories to life.

To all the future Bronze, Silver, and Gold Award Girl Scouts and others inspired by this book – Be the change you want to see in the world and remember <u>your</u> leadership matters.

MORE STORIES

Want to hear more inspiring stories from Gold Award Girl Scouts?

HeartsofGoldPodcast.com

You can watch or listen to new episodes every month.

Podcast:
https://bit.ly/3JT7x0w

YouTube:
https://bit.ly/3P5nns8

Instagram:
https://bit.ly/3JZ2JX8

9 781972 135068